LIFE'S WORK

LIFE'S WORK

FROM THE TRENCHES, A MORAL
ARGUMENT FOR CHOICE

Dr. Willie Parker

37INK

—

ATRIA

NEW YORK   LONDON   TORONTO   SYDNEY   NEW DELHI

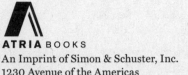

ATRIA BOOKS 37INK

An Imprint of Simon & Schuster, Inc.
1230 Avenue of the Americas
New York, NY 10020

Certain names and characteristics have been changed, whether or
not so noted in the text.

First 37 Ink/Atria Books hardcover edition April 2017

37INK/**ATRIA** BOOKS and colophon are trademarks of Simon &
Schuster, Inc.

For information about special discounts for bulk purchases, please
contact Simon & Schuster Special Sales at 1-866-506-1949 or
business@simonandschuster.com.

The Simon & Schuster Speakers Bureau can bring authors to your
live event. For more information or to book an event, contact the
Simon & Schuster Speakers Bureau at 1-866-248-3049 or visit our
website at www.simonspeakers.com.

Interior design by Dana Sloan

Manufactured in the United States of America

10 9 8 7 6 5 4 3 2

Library of Congress Cataloging-in-Publication Data
has been applied for.

ISBN 978-1-5011-5112-5
ISBN 978-1-5011-5114-9 (ebook)

LIFE'S WORK

The Women

At 6:30 a.m. on procedure day, the abortion clinic waiting room at Reproductive Health Services in Montgomery, Alabama, is as hushed as a church. Inside, beyond the bulletproof doors, the women are waiting for me, occupying every vinyl-covered chair, occasionally perched on windowsills: twenty-five, thirty, as many as fifty women sometimes. When I pass through the room in my street clothes—the uniform of sweats, baseball cap, and prescription shades that allows me to hide in plain sight—most of them won't even look up. But occasionally a woman will have heard of me, the "nice black doctor" at this clinic, and she'll meet my eyes and smile. She may believe that I'm going to get her through this, whatever "this" means to her, and hope that by making contact, with a glance, she will show me that she is an individual, with a story, and reasons, and dreams of her own.

I am here, in this crowded abortion clinic in Alabama—or Mississippi, or Georgia, where I also work—to provide abortions for women because they say they need them. I am a Christian, raised in churches right here in the South—in Birmingham, an hour-plus drive from Montgomery. In the black churches of my childhood, an unplanned pregnancy was reason enough for a public shaming, or even expulsion from church ministry. A girl who became accidentally pregnant might be forced to stand up before the congregation on a Sunday morning and beg forgiveness for her sins, while the equally sexually curious boy who helped get her pregnant sat, with his brothers and sisters in Christ, in judgment of her. Unbeknownst to me, the women in the churches of my youth must have sometimes had abortions—of course they did, legally or illegally—but no one ever spoke of them. This was the Christianity I grew up in, and it has taken me decades of emotional, spiritual, and intellectual wrestling, with my conscience and with my world, to get to the place where I am now. I remain a follower of Jesus. And I believe that as an abortion provider I am doing God's work. I am protecting women's rights, their human right to decide their futures for themselves, and to live their lives as they see fit. Today, as I write this, access to safe and compassionate abortion care is under unprecedented threat, most often from people who call themselves Christians. What I do is unfathomable to my faithful opponents, yet preserving that access is my calling. As a Christian and as a doctor, I am committed to protecting women's health.

This moral understanding came to me slowly, but it started to coalesce more than a dozen years ago when I had what I call my "come to Jesus moment" around the subject of abortion. From childhood I had long inferred that abortions were wrong, and for the first half of my career as an ob-gyn, I refused to perform them. But as I matured in both my faith and my profession, I found I was increasingly at odds with myself, an inner conflict that sat uncomfortably with me. I never questioned women's individual choices, but until I found clarity and certainty around the abortion issue—what I call the head-heart connection—I recused myself, as a practitioner, from the fight.

Since achieving that clarity of mind and fullness of heart that liberated my understanding around this work, my passion for it has doubled. I have been working as an abortion provider for more than a dozen years with increasing energy and focus. I moved back to my hometown of Birmingham to care for women living in communities like the one in which I was raised. Some of my patients, poor and black, might easily be one of my three sisters or a cousin or an aunt—others might be anyone: you, your niece, your daughter, your mother, or your best friend; many are women with some means, in the middle and upwardly mobile classes. Some of my patients have formulated strong political opinions about abortion, but more have not and merely walk through my doors because they're doing what they deem necessary for themselves. I do this work in the context of a ramped-up national crusade against it—one that promises, with a Republican president and Congress, to intensify. Calls from the antis to overturn *Roe*, to repeal the Affordable Care Act, and to defund Planned Parenthood are growing ever louder. Each one of these backward moves will not only restrict women's access to safe, affordable abortion care, but will diminish women's access to good health care in general, putting their lives and the lives of their children at risk. And poor women and women of color will bear the brunt of this political posturing by ideologues—as they always do.

Already, I have consciously put myself on the front lines. Since 2010, when right-wing extremists swept the nation's statehouses and legislatures, more than three hundred state laws have been passed aimed at restricting access to abortion—despite the fact that it is legal. In twenty-seven states, women are now forced to wait one, two, or even three days between receiving mandatory "counseling" (which often contains bogus information) and obtaining an abortion, a barrier that puts an undue burden on working women, women with children, and women who live in rural areas, requiring them to take time off work and spend additional money to travel back and forth to a clinic that may be two hundred miles from home. Fourteen states since 2010 have banned procedures after twenty weeks—a violation of *Roe*. Thirty-seven states have circumscribed "medication abortion," placing limits on patients' access to the FDA-approved pill that ends pregnancy in its early phases. And more than two dozen states have taken aim at the daily operations of the clinics themselves, placing irrational hurdles in their way with the motive of shutting them down. These laws have had the desired effect. Since 2011, more than 160 abortion clinics have closed. These laws have been passed so invisibly, so incrementally, that few have even noticed them. But they are affecting the real futures of real women by forcing them into lives they did not choose.

I think of the twenty-one-year-old woman I saw in the only open clinic in Mississippi in 2013. Born and raised in the Delta, she was home for the summer, having graduated from a Division I university, where she studied on an athletic scholarship, and she was on her way to a law school. Finding herself seven weeks pregnant, she sought my care, and I did her abortion without complication. Talking with her, I saw how clearly she saw her life. She was on the precipice, about to write a new story for herself. She would not be another dirt-poor, single mother. She would live in a world of limitless possibility, which she would create with her law degree. I sensed in her no flinching, no hesitancy, no reservation about her abortion decision. All her life, this woman had been making decisions with her future in mind, and when I saw how consequential this one was to her, my resolve to do this work increased.

When I became an abortion provider in 2002, there were twelve abortion clinics in my home state of Alabama. Now there are five. Next door, in Mississippi, there is only one. To do abortion where the need is greatest is to be itinerant, always on the road, because the distances between clinics are so great. In the car, I listen to all kinds of music: Miles and Coltrane, Kenny G and Prince, Public Enemy and the Notorious B.I.G. I am a devotee to books on tape. My time on the road has become "me time." I am always encumbered with laundry and luggage—the chores mandated by a nomad's existence. Like every busy person, I keep a fantasy future in my mind; I have purchased cooking pots and a double bass for the leisure I imagine but do not possess. Instead, I fill the gaps in my schedule with my other vocation: speaking engagements and board meetings, traveling the country like a twenty-first-century Saint Paul, preaching the truth about reproductive rights, because I have come to see that I'm the one, as the old saying goes, that I've been waiting for. As I drive long miles I become contemplative, and I reflect on my heroes: Martin Luther King Jr., Malcolm X, Sojourner Truth, and Harriet Tubman—exemplars who carried the lives and aspirations of a whole people on their backs.

My five brothers and sisters tell me they worry for my life, and I hear their concern. I understand that my commitment to this work puts me at risk. Eleven people, including four doctors, have, since the passage of *Roe v. Wade* in 1973, been assassinated for this work—killed in cold blood for the so-called sin of providing safe and legal health care for women. Rationally, I know this. But I reiterate to my siblings, and my concerned friends, my vow: I refuse to give in to fear. The truth is that I am more afraid of living a life of cowardice, of allowing any anxiety over prospective harm to keep me from my convictions. I can live with the awareness that someone might harm me. I am not so sure that I am brave enough to live with the awareness that I was too afraid to do what I knew to be right.

Though my conscience is clear and I am sure of the righteousness of my path, when I pull into the parking lot in Montgomery, or Tuscaloosa, or whatever abortion clinic I'm working in that day, I nevertheless experience an unbidden primal shiver of fear. For standing there every morning, no matter how early the hour, in the melting heat or in the driving rain, are the picketers—usually middle-aged white men who scream at me. "Murderer!" they shout. "Baby killer!" "Filthy Negro abortionist!" I do not for a second imagine that they have right on their side. I am not by nature easily intimidated. Yet their intention is to provoke me, and I do get provoked. These men incite a rage in me that I am able to quell most hours of the day. But at that early hour, sitting in my car, sometime around dawn, I am infuriated that I, who am in my fifties, gray-bearded and entirely bald, a physician with a medical degree from the University of Iowa and a master's in public health from Harvard University, have to do a version of a perp walk in order to enter my own place of work. And I am aware that, even though the intention of these protesters is to throw sticks, not stones—the truth is, you never know. One of them might come unhinged at any moment; any one of them might be carrying a gun. So while I have refused to hide, to hire a bodyguard or wear a bulletproof vest, it's impossible to escape these thoughts: *People have been assassinated for what you do. This could be your last day.* Every morning, after I turn off the ignition, I sit in my car and collect myself, to quiet myself down. I channel the courage of the civil rights legacy that I have studied, and I correlate these verbal assaults to those, much fiercer and more relentless, that Dr. King and others withstood every day. As I open the car door, I remind myself of what my mother told me when I was eight years old, the first time anyone ever called me "nigger": I should never hit someone unless he hits me first. I take a deep breath and I gather my stuff: keys, laptop, phone, bag. I do not engage. I exit my car and use the remote lock. I stand up straight, my eyes focused on the ground, and I walk, neither fast nor slow, toward my place of work.

It is never lost on me that the women in the waiting room have had to walk past these protesters, too. Even if they were escorted to the door by a cheerful young pro-choice activist with bright pink hair who carries a protective rainbow umbrella, they've heard the vitriol—different from the insults hurled at me, but no less offensive. "Think twice!" "Don't murder your baby!" The antis shout these things, as if these women had not minds of their own. As if their decision fails to merit respect. As if they were not, as most of them are, adults exercising a legal right to make a private health-care decision for themselves. (Imagine, if you will, these verbal assaults being hurled at any other person for having made any other consequential health-care choice: the decision to pursue a potentially fatal course of chemotherapy, for example. "Don't risk your life! Suicide!") The protesters find it so easy to insult the women who come to me seeking care—as if rationally deciding to terminate a pregnancy makes a woman heedless and irresponsible like a child. In my experience, the opposite is true: By the time a woman finds herself in my waiting room she has already walked a long, introspective road. She has had to take a good, hard look at her life. She has taken a world of contradictory and sometimes difficult factors into account. Whatever sex act got her here—an intercourse lit by love, passion, lust, hope, indifference, and, yes, sometimes incest or rape—is long past and obliterated now by more pressing, pragmatic concerns. It is my personal belief that the abhorrence of abortion expressed by the men who place themselves at the barricades in front of abortion clinics is actually a misplaced horror at women's sexual autonomy. It stands to reason: women's sexual independence is the thing that men have always wanted to control. But for the women in the abortion clinic waiting room, the sex itself is history and totally beside the point. They are here to pursue their lives.

Every woman sitting in one of the high-backed chairs in the Montgomery clinic has missed a menstrual period. She has peed on a stick at home or in a public restroom or at a friend's house or in a dorm and seen the result; in a flash she has had to digest how a new child will alter the future she imagines for herself. She has had to decide who she can confide in and who will judge her or disapprove and thus needs to be lied to or kept in the dark. She has confronted whatever private thoughts and yearnings she may have about her vision for her life, including deeply held and possibly heretofore unexamined ideas about professional fulfillment, love, parenthood, and God. She has had to consider the sometimes viselike practicalities that circumscribe her days: school schedules, work demands, the responsibility of caring for other children or ailing relatives, the reliable and supportive presence—or not—of the person whose sperm entered her body more than six weeks ago, her financial circumstances, her age, the limits of her own health. By the time a woman is sitting in a clinic awaiting my attention, her intention has been focused and clarified. She has figured out how to scrape together $550 if she's six weeks pregnant, or as much as $1,400 if she's further along. She has had to be true to herself, despite the fact that her decision process has been disrupted and corrupted by these new state laws requiring her to be "counseled"—by me, a credentialed doctor, or a psychotherapist—in a ginned-up "protective" encounter that often passes along to these women false or biased information about abortion disguised as scientific truth. In Mississippi, I am required to inform women that having an abortion increases their risk for breast cancer, a fraudulent fact—a lie!—for which no scientific evidence exists; I tell them what the law requires, and then, in the same breath, I explain to these women that it's simply not true. In Alabama, every abortion patient must receive a booklet called *Did You Know...*, which repeatedly uses the loaded term "unborn child" interchangeably with the more medically accurate "embryo" or "fetus"; and promotes abstinence as the surest way of birth control. If I could refuse to distribute it, I would. Instead, I hand it to the women, saying the law obliges me to do so, but you don't have to read it and you can just hand it back. By the time a woman arrives at an abortion clinic and places herself in my care, she has faced a world of judgment and found that everyone—her boyfriend, her own mother, her pastor, her best friend—has something to say.

To the point: A woman who wants to terminate her pregnancy has to make her decision in the context of a culture that shames her and, increasingly, within the constraints of laws that dramatically inconvenience her. They demean her humanity by presuming to know better than she does what her best interests are. They limit her access to clinics and doctors and they convey to her false information. The underlying assumption of all the new laws is that women can't be trusted to make their own health decisions; their doctors can't be trusted to tell them the truth; and scientific knowledge must be subverted in the name of religious truth. I strictly abide by these laws, which I believe violate human freedom, because my first priority is to continue to be able to provide abortions. If I break the law out of frustration or fury and get put out of business, the antis win.

Nevertheless, every day it's getting harder and harder for the abortion clinics in Alabama (and many other states) to stay open, because while some of the new laws are designed to interfere with a woman's decision process, others are explicitly designed to impede my ability to go to work. These are called TRAP (targeted regulation of abortion providers) laws, and they take aim at the business of abortion care, creating costly and unreasonable logistical hurdles that abortion providers must clear in order to stay in business. They require abortion doctors to obtain hospital-admitting privileges—when legislators know that no hospital will agree to give privileges to people like me, partially because many hospitals in the Bible Belt don't want the public relations headache of seeming to condone abortion by granting such privileges, and also because, practically speaking, there is no financial incentive for them to do so. (Abortion is so safe that patients very rarely require hospitalization; doctors working in outpatient abortion clinics contribute little to hospitals in the way of new "revenue streams.") The new laws require clinic hallways to be wide enough to accommodate a gurney—when the clinical need for a gurney is virtually nil. They put inefficient and unnecessary restrictions around the disposal of fetal material. For me and the other physicians who do this work, as well as for the owners of the clinics themselves, these laws require more than a mountain of paperwork. We must be tireless in our vigilance, spending untold dollars complying with every new regulation—as irrelevant to the preservation of women's health as they may be—and fighting them, in court if necessary, to ensure that a legal service remains available to all. And for her part, a woman who wants an abortion must demonstrate superhuman determination to seek it out. By the time we meet in a clinic waiting room, her resolve is often the most defining thing about her. It is matched only by my own.

Their legs jiggle on the vinyl upholstery. They look into their laps. They get lost in their phones. On a single day in Montgomery, between the hours of, say, 6:30 a.m. and noon, I will perform at least two dozen abortions, and the women who come to me are of every race: most range in age from about nineteen to nearly forty, although sometimes I see girls as young as twelve, shocked and confused by their current circumstances and waiting with their mothers. The people who pass the new laws concern themselves with fetuses, but these are humans I am caring for—real people, not merely biological organisms with the potential to become such. These individuals have full, messy, imperfect lives—and hopes and dreams that will or won't come true. Aren't they entitled to be the authors of their own stories, find their own victories and happinesses, make their own mistakes, without a congress of legislators dictating what they must do? They are college students, married women, single mothers, women without children. In a single morning I might see a woman about to enter the army; a first-grade teacher; an X-ray technician; and a zaftig, long-haired girl whose body is covered with tattoos, including one that says, *All things through Christ, who strengthens me*. Sometimes they use words like "my boyfriend" or "my husband,"

and sometimes they speak more euphemistically, as in: "this person I'm dealing with" or "I don't usually have sex." One act of sexual intercourse has brought these women here, but on the day of their abortion, the men are on the outskirts of their lives, waiting for them in trucks or SUVs they keep idling in the parking lot or by the curb. This, the abortion clinic, is a woman's world.

On the day of the procedure, I do an ultrasound to determine the gestational age of the fetus, and when I ask the woman if she wants to see the image on the screen—as I'm required in Alabama to do by law—quite a few say yes. This impulse, I believe, is the opposite of heartless or morbid. The women to whom I provide this service are clear-eyed, able to sort through all the different factors of their lives. They have the clarity they need, and that I require of them before I will perform their procedure, but—because they are human, and not robots or gods—they will never have the total certitude that the antis demand of them. They have determined at the time what is right for them and their families. And, in keeping with my ethical and Christian commitment not to make value judgments about individual women's choices, I do not interrogate them about the circumstances that brought them here (unless I sense that there's something illegal or unethical, like incest, at play, or that the woman is being coerced). But if they ask me questions, as they frequently do, I answer them as their doctor—and not as their confessor or their friend—and I give them the medical truth.

Before twenty-two weeks, a fetus is not in any way equal to "a baby" or "a child." It cannot survive outside the uterus because it cannot breathe—not even on a respirator. It cannot form anything like thoughts. Up until twenty-nine completed gestational weeks, despite what the antis may say, the scientific consensus is that it cannot feel anything like pain. I tell women that having this abortion now will not impede their future ability to have children—as many as they want—as long as their fertility persists. I do not engage in or perpetuate any of the culture's sentimental notions about the primacy of motherhood in women's lives; I regard the meeting of sperm and egg as a biological event, no less miraculous but morally and qualitatively different from a living, breathing, human life, imbued with sacredness only when the mother, or the parents, deem it so. My job, as I see it, is not to encourage or discourage women to have abortions, but rather to deploy my medical expertise in the service of their free choice, whatever that may be. And for their part, most women are relieved to be, at last, in this judgment-free zone. They understand that they have made a decision with certain consequences and, having chosen at this juncture to terminate their pregnancy, most of them are able to live, fully, with the complexity of that choice. Sometimes the women are tearful as they look at me, or at the sonogram picture, but as I learned long ago, tearfulness does not equal uncertainty. As I see it, the desire to see the sonogram image is a cry of decisiveness. *This is real. This is what I'm doing. This is what I want, having decided in this moment of my unique, individual human life not to follow a different path.*

It's later on, when they're on the table, and the weeks of pent-up anxiety turns to relief—a floodgate now that the anticipation is over—that the women start to tell their stories, unprompted. One woman says she was so sick with her first pregnancy that she had to be hospitalized; now the single parent of a nine-year-old son, she can't afford to be hospitalized again. Another plans to join the army and is already arranging to leave two very young children in the care of her parents, signing papers that make them custodians should something fatal happen to her in the line of duty. A third is following her husband's job to a big city up north and will need to resume a full-time corporate career to make ends meet. There's a recently divorced mother of three, with a one-year-old at home. There are athletes and dancers with their eye on big dreams—the Olympics, Alvin Ailey. There are women studying for degrees, hoping to become therapists, biologists, teachers, nurses. There are also drug addicts, sorority sisters, women in denial about fundamental truths in their lives, women who consent to be in destructive relationships that are impossible to understand. On occasion, I see the same woman twice in four months. Like all people everywhere, the women in these clinics are, for better or worse, merely humans doing the best they can, making this decision having taken everything they can into account. But no matter what brought them here, they do not deserve to bear the brunt of a culture's historic and dysfunctional shame. I am thinking now of a patient who sought to terminate her pregnancy because she was unmarried (though in a long-term relationship) and the leader of a Christian youth group. Feeling that she could not model "appropriate" Christian behavior under these circumstances—as a pregnant, single, Christian woman—she had an abortion instead. I didn't say this to her at the time, but it's how I felt: How much better would it have been to work through her real-life dilemma in an open and honest way for the kids she taught and not default to some rigid understanding of how Christian women ought to behave? A third of American women have had abortions, but a fraction of them are brave enough to stand up and tell their stories. I have found that when women do share their experiences of abortion, out loud, and with one another, and with the men in their lives, they do so much to push away stigma and shame—for themselves and for all women who feel silenced and blamed.

Some years ago, a dear older friend gave me a religious picture that I treasure deeply. In it, Jesus—a black Jesus—is squatting by a woman who is lying prostrate in the dirt, cowering and terrified. She is the adulteress described in the Gospel of John, about to be stoned by the authorities for violating local customs and religious laws that control the sexuality of women. In the picture, the woman is encircled by bearded men, all of whom hold stones in their hands, having decided that their prerogative is to judge and sentence her. The woman's execution is, obviously, imminent. But Jesus has intervened, and he sits by her, drawing the letters *G-R-A-C-E* in the dirt. The message of the picture, of course, is that through God's grace all is forgiven. But it struck me, as I gazed for the millionth time at the picture sitting on my desk, that maybe the picture has another meaning as well. Maybe the adulteress's name is, in fact, Grace. (In the Bible, few of the female characters actually have names.) Maybe Jesus had to make his way through the angry throng and approach the woman gently, look her in the face, and ask her name. By knowing this intimate thing, her name, and writing it in the dirt, Jesus is acknowledging not just her humanity but her individuality as well. She is a woman in general, subject to the unjust laws of her tribe, but she is also a real person, in real circumstances, and whatever they are, they do not merit public shaming or a death sentence.

So many women shoulder this self-blame that I would love nothing more than to help them cast it off. Sometimes women, having absorbed the lessons of Christian churches like the one in which I was raised, call the clinic to wonder aloud to anyone who answers the phone: "Will God forgive me?" And if I happen to be on the other end, what I say, in substance, is this: I see no reason why a woman should feel herself deserving of a separation from God because of a decision she has to make. The Jesus I love has a nonconformist understanding of his faith. He realizes that the petty rules and laws laid down by the fathers and authorities are meaningless, and that to believe in a loving God is to refuse to stand in judgment of any fellow mortal. I do not claim to be like Jesus, only to emulate him as best I can, and I do this work because I realized, a dozen years ago, that if I were in their shoes, at a crossroads and looking for compassionate support, I would want the care and attention of someone in a position to help. Rather than judge them, I give them what they came here for—as expertly, safely, quickly, and painlessly as I can—and I send them home so they can resume the lives that they want, and not lives that some authority may want for them. Performing abortions, and speaking out on behalf of the women who want abortions, is my calling. It is my life's work, and I dedicate this book to them.

CHAPTER 1

Conversion

In 2002, when I was forty-one years old, my life, by any measure, was good. I lived on the penthouse floor of a fourteen-story condo in Honolulu, Hawaii, that had floor-to-ceiling glass walls overlooking the Pacific Ocean. This meant that when I flopped onto my living room couch after a day of work and flipped through the channels on my television set, the backdrop twinkling beyond the television looked to me, having grown up in a small, tin-roofed house in Birmingham, Alabama, like something conjured in a dream—big, looping waves sparkled in the setting sun and then collapsed, frothing as their tongues and fingers reached the shore. As a kid, I had been mesmerized by the opening credits of *Hawaii Five-0*, and as a middle-aged man I still marveled daily at the fact that the view I possessed was entirely real. I had arrived in Honolulu the previous year, having accepted a faculty appointment at the University of Hawaii, and I spent my days working as a supervising physician at the Queen Emma Clinic, an outpatient clinic for indigent people, including many native Hawaiians, connected to the Queen's Medical

Center, a teaching hospital for the university. My university affiliation allowed me to see more affluent patients in a private practice,
but my main job, which occupied most of my time, was to help run
the women's health division of Queen Emma and to oversee the
work of several dozen medical residents, all in training to become
ob-gyns, as I was.

The clinic was a ten-minute walk downhill from my house,
across a highway and through a residential neighborhood, where
front gardens blossomed with fragrant orchids, birds of paradise,
and red and white blooming ginger. I frequently stopped at a convenience store on my walk to work, and picked up a Spam musubi to
eat on the way: steamed rice topped with Spam and wrapped in seaweed; occasionally, as I strolled downhill, I would catch the scent
of a rotting guava, fallen off a tree and now sweet and fermenting
in the sun, or the pungent odor of the lilikoi fruit. Ripe nectarines
grew abundantly on trees, practically begging me to pick them. The
dramatic botanical and culinary diversity of Hawaii, so different
from where I grew up, was echoed by an astonishing diversity in
the ethnic, cultural, and racial admixtures of the people called Hawaiian. As an African American, I was the rarity. The Hawaiians
have a word for black people, which is *popolo*, and for white people,
haole; the majority of people inhabiting the islands are mixed, and
the colors of brown I saw on an everyday basis made up a rainbow,
indeed—the result of Japanese, Chinese, Filipino, white, and native
Hawaiian people intermingling and procreating over generations.

Energized by the company of others and always seeking out
novel experiences, I am an extrovert by temperament. My boy-
hood had been defined by sports: I was a fairly good left fielder, and
though not as gifted as some of my peers, I was proficient enough to

be recruited my senior year of high school by a community college for its baseball team. Now I had season tickets to the university's football team, the Rainbow Warriors; the famous woman's volleyball team, the Rainbow Wahine; and when the Lakers came to Honolulu for their regular two-week preseason retreat, I frequently went to watch them play. The medical residents at the Queen Emma Clinic were a young, tight crew, more than happy to stick together and enjoy one another's company far past the grueling training hours required of them. When we clocked out at the end of a twelve- or twenty-four-hour shift, whole groups of us would retire to any bar with a sign in its window offering $2 DRINK. There, we would order pitchers of beer and gigantic platters of pupu, the Hawaiian version of soul food: pork chops, chicken wings, edamame, poke, kimchi fried rice, calamari, lomi lomi salmon—like home but with a Polynesian twist. I joke sometimes that the only people who like to set pigs on fire more than black people are Hawaiian people, and when I think of Hawaii now, one of my strongest memories is the smell of barbecue, sweet and burned, infusing the air. This was paradise, for real. I had no reason to ever want it to end.

Professionally, I was fulfilled as well. The man who had wooed me to Hawaii was an old mentor of mine, an eminent reproductive endocrinologist named Dr. Bruce Kessel, who had been an attending doctor when I was doing my residency in ob-gyn at the University of Cincinnati. During a phase of my life when I felt eternally exhausted and vulnerable, working long shifts and living in constant fear of making a fatal mistake, Bruce distinguished himself from his peers with his kindness. We reconnected several years later in Boston, when he was working at the Beth Israel hospital and I, having moved to Cambridge to get a degree in public health from

Harvard, knew no one. In Hawaii, we were a good fit. Together with Dr. Mark Hiraoka, a local Japanese-Hawaiian surfer boy turned ob-gyn, we made a sort of dream team of supervising attendings: the residents at Queen Emma were eager to work with us.

Bruce and I came from different worlds. He was the son of a prominent doctor, whereas I was fatherless and had experienced firsthand the inadequacies of the health care available to indigent people. Starting from these opposite orientations, both of us believed that the health-care system should not punish poor people, either in terms of quality of or access to care, simply because they were poor, and we both believed strongly in a holistic approach: a woman should be able to come to the Queen Emma Clinic and, in one place, get all her health needs met—to be treated for the flu and deliver her baby and get an older child vaccinated seamlessly.

On an average day, the ob-gyns at Queen Emma saw between twenty and forty patients. We did it all. We did routine gynecological care: pelvic and breast exams, Pap smears; we treated urinary tract infections, incontinence, yeast infections; we screened for STDs. We did prenatal care, monitoring pregnancy-induced diabetes and preeclampsia; and we delivered babies, doing C-sections and handling miscarriages as needed. There were all the other usual medical departments in the Queen Emma Clinic as well, so if a woman presented to us with hypertension, we might refer her to the internal medicine unit; if the internists saw a woman with abnormal vaginal bleeding, they would refer her to us. We prescribed birth control pills, inserted IUDs, and offered a fair amount of routine sex education.

As part of this menu of services, the clinic also did abortions. Bruce Kessel had been trained in abortion care as a matter of course when he was a medical resident in the early eighties. The way Bruce told it, the years after *Roe* were an exuberant time, and physicians who cared, as he did, about public health and family planning rejoiced over the freedoms and possibilities that legal abortion promised women. I was in college during those years, devoting myself to my growing passion for service by going door-to-door in my dorm, informing my college classmates about the gospel of Jesus, so it's hard for me to imagine a time when abortion rights were so enthusiastically embraced by individual practitioners—a sea change from today, when so many of my colleagues in ob-gyn are reticent to stand up for abortion, let alone to perform them themselves. But doctors of Kessel's generation, especially those who believed in family planning as a path out of poverty, sought out abortion expertise and were proud to have done so.

As a young physician, Bruce moonlighted at Planned Parenthood, which was then as it is today, the largest single provider of reproductive health services, including abortion and prenatal care, in the United States. As the senior attending and the recognized expert in fertility and menopause, he did abortions himself and trained any resident interested in learning how to do them. None of this, I might add, drew anyone's particular attention. Hawaii is, and was at the time, an extremely liberal state. Even today, Hawaii has passed none of the bans and restrictions that other state legislatures have imposed on abortion since the early 2000s—no waiting periods, no parental consent, no counseling rules—and for the vast majority of Hawaiian women living almost anywhere on the islands, abortion is easily available. As far as we were concerned, abortion was a nonissue. The clinic did them when women said they needed them, at a rate of about a hundred a year.

. . .

I, personally, didn't raise my hand to be trained in abortion care and didn't plan on doing them at all. When I was fifteen years old, I had become a born-again Christian, the result of studying the Bible under the tutelage of a charismatic and driven young Pentecostal minister in Birmingham named Mike Moore. On a sunny day in 1978, I asked for and received the indwelling of Jesus and a certainty of his love for me—a belief I hold strongly, and gratefully, to this day. This experience changed me. It gave me a sense of joy, of possibility, of a future, which I had never been able to contemplate before. But as it grew, my role as an evangelizing Christian among my friends and neighbors also placed me in a larger fundamentalist world defined by a whole lot of rules and obligations, and characterized, sometimes, by what I came to understand later as a kind of shallow conformity about what Christian people "should" and "should not" do. I lived in a world of moral certitudes: Sex outside of marriage was sinful. Unwanted pregnancy was sinful. Women were almost always the ones who had to bear the public shame of that sinfulness. So many of these rules were taken for granted in the churches of my youth, embedded in their rhetoric and principles, that though the bald facts of my own life told a feminist tale—I myself was the child of a single mother; the starting third baseman on our community baseball team was a girl—I accepted the double standard. It did occur to me to wonder about the justice of it all. *These teenage girls don't get pregnant by themselves*, I would think. But as a young person, my Christian identity was far more important to me than interrogating the inconsistencies of my faith. So even as a middle-aged man, having spent more than a decade in training as an ob-gyn, and a subsequent decade caring for women, I retained that powerful Christian identity, constricted as it was by convention and custom. Abortion fell into the category of "should nots." Consequently, as a young doctor, I made a fragile promise to myself. To uphold my professional commitment to caring for women, I would refer patients seeking abortion to doctors who would provide them. But for me, I continued to insist that providing abortion was wrong. I would not do them.

Looking back it's hard to believe, but until the spring of 2002, when I was living in bliss in Hawaii, the circumstances of my life had insulated me from having to really wrestle, in a deep and nuanced way, with the question of abortion. When I was a child, abortion wasn't a topic of any conversation, polite or otherwise. When I was a young teenager, encountering Jesus for the first time, the political terms "pro-life" and "pro-choice" did not exist, nor did the milieu that forced people to pick a side. And though through Mike Moore, who was first my baseball coach and then my pastor and friend, I became enraptured with the idea of God's radical, egalitarian love, I was not yet in possession of the intellectual tools to unpack or query the fundamental sexism embedded in the ancient Scripture, or to discover for myself a more nuanced, or feminist, vision of justice. Now I see the Bible as it was written: the inspired word of God, but also a historical document preserving the ancient hegemony of men; starting with Eve, women are always thrown under the bus when it suits the men in power to do so. But the way I understood Christianity as a young person was literalistic, strictly black and white. The churches I was raised in were patriarchal. The father was the head of the family, just as Jesus was the head of the church. I tried, as Mike taught me, to emulate Jesus by upholding a biblical standard of sexual purity—and I did. I did not have sex until I was twenty-one, and so, unlike the other teenagers in my neighborhood, I never had to face the actual fear of an accidental pregnancy, nor the heart-thrumming anxiety of what that pregnancy might mean—not just to the future of the woman or girl in question, but to me, as an equal participant in the conception. My life was all about serving God. Having chosen heaven, I didn't want to risk the chance that I might go to hell.

Abortion first entered my vision only abstractly, as a news event, with the rise of the Moral Majority, the very vocal and political Christian constituency whose anti-abortion rhetoric helped elect Ronald Reagan in 1980. I had just left Birmingham for college when slogans such as "Life begins at conception" began to be bandied about. And my first effort at grappling with abortion was intellectual, too—as removed from the real lives of real women as I was at the time. In my first year at Berea College, in 1981, I wrote a paper about abortion for a required freshman course called Issues & Values; my professor, who had formerly been a Catholic priest, suggested the topic to me. In those days, I traveled almost exclusively in fundamentalist Christian circles. No one I knew talked about having abortions, and I had no clue where one of my classmates might get an abortion in central Kentucky, had she decided she needed one. Committed personally to sexual abstinence, I was totally oblivious to the real-life circumstances that might lead a woman to that decision. And so I did not question the rigid Christianity I had learned at home, which was perpetuated by my Christian friends and mentors at school. I held fast to my understanding of the moral rights and wrongs concerning the sacredness of sex and marriage, and the potency of God's will. In my paper, I called abortion a "life-ending process." As a believer in the healing power of prayer, I hoped women in this undesirable situation might enter into their decision making "prayerfully." God, I hoped, would find a way. About fetuses and their viability, I had no opinion at all. As a child in Birmingham, my friends and I used to watch cows and dogs mate. We knew where babies came from, but we never moralized about the process.

I learned a black-and-white faith, but I am not a black-and-white person. Even in college, my love for science began to chip away at some of the absolutist claims of my faith. In medical school at the University of Iowa, I even began to see how abortion might be regarded as necessary health care for women. Partly, my own personal world had expanded. In the years since my Issues & Values paper, I had become sexually active, and for the first time in my life had to cope with the emotionally fraught aftermath of a broken condom. My girlfriend at the time, an ambitious woman with her sights set on a very competitive residency, made me promise, tearfully, that if she became pregnant I would support her decision to terminate the pregnancy and not ask her to bring a fetus to term. She had worked hard her whole life and wanted to become an orthopedic surgeon more than anything. Moved by her anxiety that I might fail to be a loving support to her, and by my own strong desire to defy the stereotype of the sexually irresponsible black man (even though nothing in my personal history indicated that I might conform to it), I easily agreed—an agreement that cost me nothing because she did not become pregnant. Then, in my third year of medical school, as part of my coursework, I decided to observe abortions on my ob-gyn rotation for the simple reason that I was curious. I had no part in performing them, but for the first time, I took the patients' medical histories and was in the room with the doctor where the procedures occurred, and I remember understanding, profoundly, that these women were like me. They were mostly college students—eighteen, nineteen, or twenty years old. I was twenty-five. In the moment, they were choosing to pursue their educations over parenthood. Their decisions resonated with me: they made sense. The moral absolutes that I had learned in church began further to erode.

It is a testament to the strength of my Christian faith that it took me so long to revise my stance on abortion, for the seeds of my personal revolution were in me from childhood. But even after medical school, when I saw that I related to and empathized with the women who sought out abortion care, and even in Hawaii, where attitudes around abortion were relatively relaxed, I still refused to do them myself. Part of this was circumstance. At the University of Cincinnati, where I did my residency, abortion care was not offered as part of the program, and the university hospital did not openly perform abortions at all. The first abortion clinic bombings post-*Roe* had occurred in Cincinnati in 1978, and I believe that, situated as the hospital was in a conservative, Republican city, its administrators had decided not to take up the fight. So even though I was being trained to provide health care for women, I saw only one abortion performed during the whole time I was there: my attending physician, Dr. Paula Hillard, who has since become a friend, discreetly did a fourteen-week procedure in the operating room and invited me to observe. That observation was the extent of my experience with the procedure. As a young doctor, it was easy for me to say I wouldn't do abortions, because the fact was, I *couldn't* do them. I didn't know how.

Later, when I worked as an ob-gyn in general practice in a community health center in medically underserved Merced, California, circumstances again conspired to protect me from the conflicts that were rising in my own conscience. There were no abortion providers within fifty miles of the Golden Valley Health Center women's clinic, so every patient seeking an abortion had to be referred away. For almost the entire time that I was a practicing ob-gyn there, I had the luxury of holding on to my unexamined Christian morals, uncontested by circumstance. I could tell myself that I was doing good work, helping poor women deliver healthy babies, and providing birth control to teenagers and working against domestic violence. But on the question of abortion, I could continue to absolve myself of having to take responsibility for my own inaction, pointing to the authorities or circumstances or laws that barred me from doing battle with myself. I was not pro-life. I believed in a woman's right to choose. But I was complicit with anti-abortion forces in that I did not place myself on the front lines.

. . .

In March of that year in Hawaii, however, the line I had drawn was getting harder and harder to defend. The board of the Queen Emma Clinic had recently hired a new chief administrator, a man I will call here Dr. Sweet. He was a lovely person, Hawaii born and bred, with a gentle, nonconfrontational demeanor, and I knew that he was a Bible-believing Christian, as I was. He began his tenure like a lamb, deferential, but his intention soon became startlingly clear. Within months of his arrival, Dr. Sweet let it be known that the Queen Emma Clinic would no longer be providing abortion services to its patients. His rationale was, in my opinion—then and now—misbegotten.

It was the beginning of the George W. Bush era, and anti-abortion sentiment was at a peak. Dr. Sweet told us that if we continued to offer abortion services to patients, our Title X money—federal funds that support the family planning needs of poor people, excluding abortion—would be at risk. This was not true. Family planning clinics receiving Title X grants have merely to have rigorous accounting practices to show a separate funding stream for their abortion services. (Planned Parenthood clinics still receive Title X money; they just can't use it to support their abortion practice.) But Dr. Sweet had been raised in fundamentalist Christian churches, as I was, and he was now the target of zealous political activism by anti-abortion forces who were telling him, from the pulpit, and on Christian television and radio, that "abortion is murder." Sweet was no fanatic, but a gentle, traditionally minded man disinclined to question the religious authorities in his life, a person who hoped more than anything to discharge his professional duties within the context of his Christian faith. The prominent spokespeople for his faith were telling him that abortion was evil, and, in my opinion, he chose to believe them. I understood his dilemma—no one understood it better than I—but I vehemently disagreed with his action. In fact, I was surprised at how fast indignation boiled up within me. This was a public hospital serving an indigent population. I believed, based on long years in the field of public health, that the services we offered should be based on the needs of our patients and not subjected to the religious beliefs of the doctor.

Dr. Sweet's edict coincided with a time of a dramatic change in the way anti-abortion activists were waging their war against abortion rights. The 1990s had been characterized by violence and hatred: threats, bombings, assassinations of clinic workers, and massive demonstrations aimed at the Supreme Court and, more broadly, at the hearts and minds of the public. As a medical resident I had been dimly aware of this war—the Planned Parenthood clinic in Cincinnati had been firebombed in December 1985, five years before I arrived there, and the abortion doctor David Gunn was assassinated in Florida in my final training year—but until Dr. Sweet's intervention, I thought of the battle as raging "out there." Partly because ob-gyns are trained to concentrate on obstetrics, I was paying attention to delivering babies. And partly, I did not feel pressed to wrestle with my own uncertainties about abortion because there had been no need. Here, in Hawaii, abortion was so available, so accessible, no one was counting on me to take a stand.

But as Sweet's decision showed, the terms of engagement were changing. Instead of focusing their efforts on overturning *Roe*, the antis began stealthily chipping away at abortion access on the state and local level, arguing that fetuses had "rights" equal to kindergartners learning to tie their shoes. Overnight, it seemed—and at around the same time that Dr. Sweet was making his assault on abortion at the Queen Emma Clinic—the antis had masterfully changed the terms of the debate, turning the vitriol of previous decades into something like civic righteousness. The war on abortion rights began to be waged in terms of "human rights." The living, breathing women who carried those fetuses in utero were cast as less than fully human—either as criminals, on the one hand, or mentally incompetent on the other—and thus not in possession of any rights at all. It was not lost on me, an African American man from Birmingham, Alabama, descended from slaves, that new legislation aimed at telling women what they might and might not do

with their own physical bodies looked a whole lot like men own-
ing women's bodies. It was Eve being thrown under the bus all over
again.

Upon hearing of the imminent change at Queen's, six female
residents whose training I oversaw decided they would rebel. They
would circumvent Sweet's decision by creating a small abortion
practice at another hospital across town. Under their plan, patients
who came to Queen Emma seeking abortion care would be referred
to their practice (among others), where Sweet had no jurisdiction.
Their determination, and their fast move to action, filled me with
awe. The life of a medical resident isn't easy. You're on call every
fourth night, and generally exhausted. These women could have
been far more passive, complicit. After work, they could have con-
templated the orchids blossoming in their own front yards and their
surfboards languishing on their back porches and thought, *I'm in
a great residency program at a great teaching hospital and I am
being worked to the bone. Let me take a break.* But they didn't. They
took on extra work on behalf of the women they wanted to serve. So
when they asked me if, as their faculty adviser, I would lend support
to their new initiative, I enthusiastically said yes. Without thinking,
I took a stand.

Separately, Bruce Kessel and I were exploring solutions within
the hospital's management. This was an abuse of authority, we
thought, and it violated our first principles. How could we conscien-
tiously say we cared for all aspects of a woman's health if we failed
to provide this crucial service? How could we reasonably say that
our care of poor women was nondiscriminatory? We went to our
boss, Dr. Richard Friedman. Could Dr. Sweet do this? we asked.
Dr. Friedman said yes, he could. Dr. Sweet was within his rights to

shut the service down. The only compromise that could be struck was this: we could perform abortions in our own private practices, which were not under the jurisdiction of the Queen Emma Clinic. This was a small concession, and worthless: the indigent women who came to Queen's had no insurance and could not afford to pay out of pocket for the services of a private physician.

I could no longer defer my ethical engagement. I believed that Dr. Sweet was changing the rules as a prerogative of his power, and then presenting the change in the guise of responsible and visionary stewardship. Bruce and I felt that our patients were entitled to abortions if they wanted them—and they had been receiving abortion care, without controversy or comment, for thirty years. Queen Emma represented an ideal of integrated care for women who were abjectly poor. I didn't realize how ideal until I saw how they would suffer under this change. They were at the Queen Emma Clinic because they had nowhere else to go. To me, it wasn't acceptable to deny them a safe and legal procedure. It wasn't right.

In retrospect, I had already deferred this moment for far too long. I had refused to perform abortions out of loyalty to my Christian identity, but I had evolved a great deal since my Christian conversion, and other identities had long since grown up beside it. At forty-one, I was a Christian, yes, but I was also a doctor, a health-care provider for poor women, and a man who loves women—in partnership, in friendship, at work, and in my family. I didn't do abortions, but I had seen enough patients in my dozen-plus years as an ob-gyn and had grown close to enough women in my life to know that all kinds of women sometimes find themselves pregnant and unable or unwilling to raise a child. Sometimes these instances are so striking that it's impossible not to see abortion as a palliative solution to psychic pain. Before coming to Hawaii, I had worked for three years as a government doctor in Merced, where there was a shortage of medical care, and one day, a young woman, eighteen or nineteen years old, came into my office. She was alone, having driven herself to the clinic from her home, some twenty miles away. This woman had become pregnant through incest by her father, a very controlling, overbearing—and religious—man. She was Latina, from a family of migrant workers, raised in a community defined by patriarchal hierarchy. Because she was not a minor or dependent, I had no legal duty to report this tragic situation, and I knew enough about her cultural context to understand that involving law enforcement without her consent could make this woman's daily circumstances even worse. In an extreme sense, this woman was doing what was expected of her, which was to live in her father's house until she moved, ultimately, into her husband's. In light of these facts, her bravery—coming to me by myself, and seeking my help—struck me as extraordinary. I referred her to the closest clinic I could, which was about fifty miles away, but I remember thinking that if I had the skills to do her abortion, I would do it, right then and there.

. . .

That afternoon in Hawaii, upon learning that Dr. Sweet's ruling was final, I walked home from the clinic, seething and blind to all the usual glories around me. Furious and frustrated, I took the elevator to the fourteenth floor, changed out of my scrubs and into shorts, and sank onto the couch, mindlessly flipping through television channels. My self-doubt circled around on itself. I was thinking about my medical residents, the young doctors who were already cooking up a plan to provide abortion care at another hospital within walking distance of my condo. They inspired me. I saw their defiance as just, and revolutionary. How could I match their clarity of purpose? How might I reconcile my commitment to my Christian faith with what I saw as an arbitrary abuse of power, the very definition of injustice? I had long been in the habit of listening to audiotapes to settle me—I loved to listen to the Trappist monk Thomas Merton on contemplative prayer; the Kentucky novelist Wendell Berry's reflections on the interconnectedness of life; and the popular Christian theologian C. S. Lewis. Recently, I had been working my way through a collection of sermons by Dr. King himself. I had long found comfort and inspiration in his words, and that evening I turned to him.

You might call Dr. King my personal saint; he was, in 2003, and he is today, my conscience's mentor and its guide. As a young man, Dr. King had aspired to be a physician, and when I myself was choosing my path, it was King's conviction, articulated in his 1963 book *Strength to Love*, that persuaded me that a life devoted to science posed no contradiction to my strong Christian faith. "Science gives man knowledge, which is power," he wrote. "Religion gives man wisdom, which is control. The two are not enemies." It would not be too much to say that with words Dr. King wrote when I was just one year old, I was persuaded that my two great interests, science and religion, did not conflict.

Dr. King had been blessing me long before I came of age or reckoned with my own ambition. Although I had no awareness of it at the time, I had grown up in the hot center of the civil rights movement, in a segregated neighborhood in Birmingham, and had gone, until third grade, to a segregated school. Carlton Reese, who composed many of the songs that marked the movement as a homegrown product of

the African American church, grew up two doors down from me, and
Dr. King wrote some of the most resonant, indelible words of the civil
rights campaign from a jail cell not ten miles from where I grew up:
"Injustice anywhere is a threat to justice everywhere."

I was the very child he hoped to deliver from racial discrimina-
tion. I was the young boy whose future he was marching for. I was in
kindergarten when he was assassinated on the balcony of the Lor-
raine Motel in Memphis, Tennessee, and I remember the grown-
ups buzzing about it in church-school kindergarten that day: "They
killed Dr. King! They killed Dr. King!" At the time, we got all our
news from black talk radio (there was no programming on television for black people), and I remember the next day hearing on the
radio that black folks should leave their porch lights on in solidarity
and in remembrance of him, an allusion to the instructions God
gave the Israelites in Exodus before inflicting upon the Egyptians
the tenth and final plague: *Mark your front door with lamb's blood
and I will pass over your houses and spare the lives of your children.*
We all struggled to pay our electricity bills, and I couldn't believe
that people's porch lights were on in the daytime. But even though
many of my neighbors were working too hard, too absorbed in the
grind of their daily lives, and fundamentally too cautious to join
Dr. King's revolution, we were, in a very real sense, his children. He
was our Moses—taken from us in the prime of his life without ever
seeing the promised land.

My audiotape collection was, by serendipity, queued up that day
to "I've Been to the Mountaintop," Dr. King's final sermon, which
I'd heard dozens, maybe hundreds, of times. I could quote whole
sections of it, word for word, from memory. "For when people get
caught up with that which is right and they are willing to sacrifice

for it," he said, "there is no stopping point short of victory." On that afternoon, however, as I wrestled with the fact that certain women were being denied the health-care services they sought because of someone else's idea of what they should do, I heard the sermon with new ears. As he nears the final, rousing lines of the speech—"Let us rise up tonight with a greater readiness"—Dr. King recounts a story from the gospels, one that every Christian knows by heart, one that I myself was taught in Sunday school.

In the story of the Good Samaritan, a man is lying, wounded and helpless, on the Jericho Road, having been beaten up: He "fell in with thieves," as Dr. King put it. Two men, a priest and a Levite (the first obligated to help others by vocation and the second presumed to have a tribal or family affiliation with the victim), bypass the man, leaving him lying in the road. Finally, a Good Samaritan— a man with no good reason to give assistance—"got down from his beast, decided not to be compassionate by proxy," as Dr. King said. The Samaritan "administered first aid, and helped the man in need." Of the three, only the Samaritan was great, Jesus said.

I closed my eyes as Dr. King's words began to fill my heart. In his sermon, Dr. King begins to speculate, almost sardonically, on the reasons the first two might have hurried past a man as wounded and desperate as the traveler was. Maybe they were frantically busy and late for a church meeting. Or maybe they were following a religious edict that required priests and Levites not to contaminate themselves by touching another human body in advance of a religious ritual. Or maybe they were devoted to a different, broader kind of civic assistance—perhaps they had joined a committee to improve the safety of travelers, "a Jericho Road Improvement Association," as Dr. King put it. "Maybe they felt it was better to deal with the problem from the causal root, rather than to get bogged down with an individual effect."

As the sun was going down outside my penthouse apartment, the undulations of Dr. King's voice soothed me. And then he got to his point. "It's possible that those men were afraid," he said. The Jericho Road is a dangerous road, and in Jesus's day, it was teeming with thieves. It's possible, Dr. King suggests, that the priest and the Levite were worrying, first and foremost, about their own skins and wished not to draw unwelcome attention or danger to themselves by dismounting from their animals or lingering over a person disabled by circumstance. "Or it's possible that they felt that the man on the ground was merely faking," part of a scheme to lure unwitting, soft-hearted travelers into an ambush. The priest and the Levite passed the man by because their first thought, Dr. King suggested, was fear for themselves: "If I stop to help this man, what will happen to me?" What made the Good Samaritan good, in Dr. King's interpretation, was that he reversed the question. "If I do not stop to help this man, what will happen to him?"

It was like a punch, all at once, in my spiritual gut. The Scripture came alive and it spoke to me. For the Samaritan, the person in need was a fallen traveler. For me, it was a pregnant woman. The earth spun, and with it, this question turned on its head. It became not: Is it right for me, as a Christian, to perform abortions? But rather: Is it right for me, as a Christian, to refuse to do them? And in that instant, I understood that I, like the Levite and the priest, had been afraid—afraid of what my Christian brothers and sisters might think of me, of what my pastors and relatives in Birmingham might say, of what the social or political consequences of fully embracing the cause of abortion might be. I had been worried, if truth be told, about tarnishing my professional reputation. I was already speaking out on domestic violence and sexual assault. Wasn't that enough? My love for my cushy situation was fighting for its life against my conscience—and my conscience prevailed. I had erred too long on the side of caution—just as I did when, in my senior year of college, I declined to join a campus-wide protest against the school's investments in South Africa, afraid that someone might develop a negative opinion about me and I would ruin my chances for medical school, a demurral I regret deeply to this day. Now I saw, without doubt or fear or ambivalence, that it was appropriate, even ethical, for me to provide this care. More: that having understood this, it would be inappropriate, even cowardly, for me to be contented to sit by as other people did the work.

From that moment, not providing abortions and not living out my convictions would have been a fate worse than death. Once I understood that the faithful approach to a woman in need is to help her and not to judge her or to impose upon her any restriction, penalty, or shame, I had to change my life. The words of the Holocaust survivor and peace activist Elie Wiesel reverberated within me. "Our lives," he said, "no longer belong to us alone. They belong to those who need us desperately."

The next day I went to Bruce Kessel and told him I wanted to learn how to do abortions. Within two years I was gone from Hawaii, training full-time in abortion care, and committed in my effort, which continues to this day, to be true to Dr. King's idea of justice. I do not remember feeling an ounce of remorse or regret at my decision—only sorrow that I hadn't come to it sooner. On that day, I decided to exercise Christian compassion not by proxy but with my own capable hands.

CHAPTER 2

Grace of God

I grew up in a community called Wylam, in a neighborhood that back in the day had been called Number 8—a collection of unheated shacks arranged in a grid atop a small hill. Number 8 was a residential community of workers' housing, created by the Tennessee Coal, Iron and Railroad Company in western Jefferson County, Alabama, at the beginning of the twentieth century to accommodate the African American coal miners who worked—sometimes for pennies, and sometimes, if they were conscripts, for nothing at all—in the tunnels hundreds of feet underground. Technically, these miners were not slaves, but their status and the terms of their employment met nearly every definition of the word. The mines were closed by the time I was born, but Wylam still had the feel of a company town. Everyone I knew was descended from someone who had worked in the mines (many men in the neighborhood still worked in mines nearby), and everyone, except for the people who owned the store and lived on a street we called "the white people's quarters," was black. My grandfather, Allen Parker Sr., had been a coal miner, but by the time I knew him he was retired and already old—a tall, stern, caramel-colored man of seventy, thin but invincible in my six-year-old mind. I loved him with my whole heart. When I was very young he was my primary caregiver, looking after me while my mother worked, and I would spend long days with him, walking into the country and scavenging garbage heaps in the early mornings, looking for treasures to take home—a chair that needed refinishing, a washer with a broken motor—and watching soap operas in the afternoons. He called them "the stories": *General Hospital*, *One Life to Live*, *Guiding Light*, and *The Edge of Night*. My grandfather loved the stories and he loved sweets—cakes, banana pudding, and, especially, fruit-flavored sodas.

"Boy," he would say to me when I was eight or nine years old, "go get me a Coca-Cola."

"What flavor?" I would ask.

"Grape," he'd answer. When I returned with the soda, I'd beg him to "save me the bottle," by which he knew I meant a swig at the bottom, and he always did.

My grandfather owned his house, a small wood home with a front porch near the top of the hill, and until I was eleven, my three older siblings—Juanita, Mary, and Fred—lived full-time with him. I officially lived in a smaller house up the hill with my mother, Jackie Parker; her husband, George Lambert; and, eventually, my younger sister, Earnestine. But it was my grandfather who was in charge of me while my mother worked as a domestic "over the mountain," as we used to call the suburb where the white people lived. The father of the family for which she worked was a dentist we called Mr. Sammy. The mother was Miss Pat. And because we never had a car, Mr. Sammy would come by our house in his red Mustang each morning to give my mother a ride to work. I would hop in the back, and Mr. Sammy would drop me at my grandfather's house before they continued on to his house. Mr. Sammy and Miss Pat had a son named Lance, who was about my age. Sometimes Lance would be in the backseat, too, and I understood that my mother spent her days caring for Lance instead of for me. Mr. Sammy was kind, in his way. My mother had poor dentition, related to poverty, a lack of regular dental care, and a habit of incessant smoking, and Mr. Sammy decided at one point to fit my mother with dentures, and pulled out all her teeth. But the dentures never fit right, and my mother never wore them; in my memories of her, she never has teeth. For the rest of her short life—she died at fifty-four—my mother chewed all her food with her gums, which were as hard as steel. I once mocked her gently for not having teeth and she told me to put my finger in her mouth. She clamped down like a snapping turtle and made her point.

I was born on October 18, 1962, and am the fourth of my mother's six children. Earnestine was born four years after me, in 1966, and Steve, the baby, in 1971. Each of us has a different father, and I never knew mine, by name or by sight. My surname, Parker, is my mother's maiden name and can be traced back only as far as my great-grandfather Tom, a slave who, as family legend has it, lived to be one hundred five years old and hailed from Sylacauga, Alabama, a rural town located halfway between Montgomery and Birmingham. Parker was doubtless the slave owner's name. Maybe some Parkers still live around Sylacauga, but I have never looked for them. Sometimes I refer to myself, half in jest, as "a colored boy from Birmingham," because that's what my birth certificate says. According to that official document, my sex at birth was male, my mother's race was "colored," and the space for the father's name was blank.

George Lambert was Earnestine's father, and until he and my
mother split, I assumed in the unthinking way of a child that he was
my father, too. He was nice enough to me, but a drinker, a manual
laborer who borrowed against his paycheck and was never able to
meet our material needs. He and my mother seldom fought—but
when they did, they fought about me. One weekend afternoon when
I was six or seven years old, Daddy George was charged with looking after me while my mother was at work. I remember getting hungry and deciding that while he was sleeping off his liquor, I would
cook myself an egg. Because we had no electricity in our house, we
cooked our food on a woodstove we had to light with a match. When
my mother came home from work that night, they had a great row,
my mother accusing Daddy George of being negligent. "He could
have burned the house down!" she said. They took their argument
out to the front porch, and when, in her protective fury, my tall,
strong mother pushed Daddy, he fell off the porch and broke his
arm. A few years later, when I was eleven, my mother and the only
father I knew split up. We—Momma, Earnestine, two-year-old
Steve, and I—all moved in with my grandfather. I was expected to
share a bed with my grandfather and my brother Fred, but until we
got bunk beds, I preferred to sleep on the floor.

Zebra babies can flat-out run within an hour of being born, because if they can't, they're dead. We were like zebras, so poor we
didn't know how poor we were, and tough and independent because
there wasn't any other way to be. No one in my family had ever been
to college. No one did anything—or expected to do anything—but
menial, physical work. We used food stamps to get our food, Medicaid to pay what health bills we had, and were blessed with shelter because Granddaddy owned our house. My grandfather died in

1974, and soon thereafter my mother had to stop working because of her health. She had what we called "bad nerves"—officially diagnosed as manic depression. Twice, she was hospitalized after psychotic breaks, but she was able to control her mental health with regular outpatient care; as I learned later in medical school, the frequency and severity of her attacks diminished as she cycled toward stability. She also had severe hypertension and early onset peripheral vascular disease, known in layman's terms as hardening of the arteries: when I was a junior in high school, her right leg was amputated. With my mother not working, we had no income to speak of. We lived on her disability benefits, some Social Security from Daddy George (he and my mother never legally divorced), and whatever the rest of us could scrape together. It was barely enough. One year, my mother arranged for me to live with my sister Juanita, who had moved with her husband to a rough housing project called the Brickyard—it was so much nearer to school than my grandfather's house, and too often we didn't have the daily bus fare for the round-trip, even though it was just thirty cents each way.

Yet, even then I wasn't unhappy. We had no objective perception of our own poverty because we had nothing to compare it to. Most of our neighbors were poor or working-class. We never doubted our mother's love for us, and we saw how much she sacrificed to give us everything she could. We were a family, and we looked after one another as best we could. My grandfather had a plum tree and a peach tree behind his house, and a little garden where he grew peppers, greens, string beans, cabbage, tomatoes, corn, strawberries, grapes, and a row of sugarcane, the raw taste of which I did not like. Down the hill, in a patch of scrub, he had a pen where he kept hogs. It was one of my jobs to slop the hogs after dinner, a job I hated because the slop pail was heavy and the hogs stank. Still, the budding scientist in me was intrigued by their behavior. (Granddaddy always cautioned me to be careful or the hogs would eat me: I should slop them and come right back.) Once a year he and the other men in the neighborhood would slaughter a hog, hitting it first over the head with a sledgehammer, and then shooting it in the brain with a rifle. We ate that hog "from the rootie to the tootie," as we playfully said.

Number 8 was a village. Everybody knew everybody. Down our street lived Miss Ceola, who sold the ice pops she made in her freezer to neighborhood kids for a nickel apiece. We called them "beebop." Next door lived Miss Edna White and her daughter, Arlene, six years older than me, who taught me how to ride a bike by putting me on the seat and letting me steer and pedal while she controlled the balance. All the mothers were fierce with their own children, and, by unstated collective agreement, fierce with one another's kids as well. You didn't dare tease the neighbor's dog, because if you did, the neighbor would whip you—and then she'd bring you home to your mother, who would whip you again. There was no such thing as double jeopardy in my neighborhood. My own mother never hesitated to use corporal punishment on us—most often with a switch, but sometimes a belt or a shoe. My brother Fred still laughs when he remembers that shoe, so innocuous a household thing, but unforgettable when my mother was angry.

I remember one time, when I was about fourteen years old, my mother asked me to rake the yard. A neighbor named Mr. Pat was sitting out on his high porch, just across the street, watching us from no more than twenty feet away. And—I could never figure out what compelled me—I talked back to my mother in some insolent way. I said something like "I said I'd do it and I'll do it." And Mr. Pat looked at my mother, like *What are you going to do about this?* And my mother looked at Mr. Pat and me. And then I looked at Mr. Pat and my mother. And then my mom grabbed me. She slammed me down on the porch and put her knee on my chest. She said, "As much as I go through to feed you, as much as I take off my back and give to you. And you're going to talk to me like that? Nigger, I will kill you." I perceived all the love in her use of the N-word and none of the epithet. There must be a manual that all black mothers have with sayings in them. And one of them is "I brought you here and I'll take you out." It hurt my feelings that my mother said she'd kill me. It did. But that pain didn't take hold or linger. I never felt that my mother was being unduly harsh, because I understood that there was nothing she wouldn't do for me.

. . .

Despite the fact that our lives were defined and constrained by our very limited means, I grew up with a powerful and constant sense that I was different. Partly, this was because I appeared to be fragile. I am a large man now, five feet eleven inches tall and 250 pounds—ex-linebacker size—but I was small as a kid, skinny and frail, and late to cross puberty's threshold. At the poor people's clinic where we saw the doctor, a nutritionist once told my mother I was underweight and recommended she give me rice cereal for breakfast, fattened with sugar, butter, and condensed milk. I loved it: rice pudding for breakfast! Though small, I was clever enough to evade the bullies at school. At home, I was less successful. I scrapped constantly with my brother Fred, who looks like a supersize version of me, and he would toss me around like a rag or a ball. Both of us would get whipped for fighting, but Fred ran afoul of our mother more often, and she usually took my side.

Also, I was asthmatic from an early age, sometimes wheezing and coughing until I could barely breathe. This condition abated as I grew older, enabling me to play sports as a teenager, and my mother was vigilant to my condition. She administered theophylline when needed, and sought out home remedies when she could: an older cousin of mine sometimes stopped by the house to give me a dried herb to smoke. She dug it up in the woods, and we called it "rabbit tobacco." I can understand now that it had natural bronchio-dilating effects. Despite these home remedies, the asthma attacks were often so severe that my mother and I would find ourselves a ride downtown to the emergency room at Children's Hospital so I could get injections of epinephrine in my shoulder. The white doctors were kind and patient, for I frequently needed repeated intramuscular shots before my wheezing would subside, and my strongest memory of those hospital visits is that they gave me Cokes. I know now that asthma disproportionately afflicts children who live in poverty, residing as they do in places where air quality is low. We lived less than one hundred yards from slag heaps generated by U.S. Steel—gigantic piles of gravel that were the by-products of steel production. And in certain seasons, my grandfather's house was full of roaches and mice, which would come out from behind the walls while we slept. One night, when I was in high school and up late, watching television and talking on the phone, I caught fourteen mice in traps I baited with bacon and peanut butter, one after another.

I also got extra attention from the adults in my world because I was perceived as smart. An early reader, I whiled away long afternoons at a neighbor's house, devouring her massive collection of comic books. I was always reading above grade level, from first grade on, and in the third grade the teacher, Miss Orton, gave me and one other boy advanced assignments, encouraging us to read about the Greek gods—Zeus, Hera, Aphrodite, Athena—which I loved. I helped younger children with their schoolwork, and my friends' parents took on the role of encouraging me. "That boy right there," they'd say. "He's really smart. He's going to be something someday. Keep it up Willie James."

Because of all this, I was singled out for additional responsibility. People in the neighborhood knew they could trust me to run errands—to go to the store and return in good time with exactly the items they'd asked me for and the correct change, or to cash a check and stop by the electric company to pay a bill. In thanks, I'd get a nickel, or a quarter, so I could buy myself a candy bar, or a honey bun. I learned how to drive when I was a teenager, so even though I had no license, I frequently gave our neighbor, whom we called "Lady," a lift to the airport when she went on trips with her social club, and then drove her car home and carefully parked it in her driveway and watched over it until it was time to pick her up again.

This sense of specialness was reinforced. It became who I was: my mother's good child. Even today, with my mother gone for almost thirty years, my siblings refer to me that way—the good one, the one who always does the right thing. So while Fred was popular and cool, playing basketball all day and partying and hanging out with young men, some of whom would eventually go to jail, I tried, as much as I could, to stay out of trouble. Sure, my buddies and I might steal a watermelon from a neighborhood garden, crack it on the ground, and eat it right there on a hot summer's day, but if any one of the boys in my group suggested that we jack a car or rob a store, I would always ask for a ten-minute head start wherein I'd ditch them and disappear into another book. I don't drink and have never in my life smoked weed; in high school I was the guy the pretty, popular girls told their secrets to, confiding in me about boys with whom they were sleeping—or hoped to. I remember one night driving around with Fred and one of his friends in Fred's yellow Charger, a muscle car he'd bought in 1979. The windows were rolled up, and they were both smoking reefer, the interior of the car filling with billows of smoke. Determined not to get high, I held my breath until I couldn't any longer, and then I broke down and opened the window. "Close the window!" Fred yelled from the front. "You're letting out all the good smoke!" My mother figured out early on that while whippings would make me behave, another tactic worked even better. She would say, "I expected that out of Fred. But I'm disappointed in you." It pressed my buttons. I was a pleaser, and nothing mattered to me more than my mother's high opinion.

In retrospect I see a winning childhood—materially challenged, but culturally rich—but I also understand deeply the tremendous power of community approval and judgment that my patients have to weigh as they ponder their abortion decision. I know what it is like to be thought less of, and to feel frustrated that, despite your best efforts, you can't get ahead. I have come to make sense of my life through this truism I once heard: Life is best understood by looking backward, but it has to be lived forward. Providence, hard work, and good judgment have positioned me to walk my current path, and I now feel that I have the perspective of the Old Testament character Joseph, who, as a prosperous adult, encountered his older brothers, who had jealously left him in a ditch to die. They thought he would be bitter, but he was not: he saw that God made his past circumstances for good, and that through them he was enabled to save many lives. I am absolutely convinced that everything in my upbringing has prepared me for my abortion work. I say this because I believe what they say: Experience is not what happens to you. Experience is what you do with what happens to you. All that has happened to me fuels the compassion I need to do my work, for in my interactions with the women I treat, I am constantly mindful of the fact that but for the grace of God, there go I.

CHAPTER 3

———

"That Girl"

Every Sunday until I was twelve years old, my mother sent me to First United Missionary Baptist Church, on Seattle Street in Wylam. It was a brick building on the edge of Number 8, with a stumpy little steeple that barely indicated the sky. First there was Sunday school and then there was church, and our mother's rule was that we couldn't play outside unless we'd been to church. So we went. It wasn't a hardship, because I loved it—it gave me more opportunities to learn and achieve. I was a junior usher, and I was in the choir, and because I was deemed to be smart, I was given extra verses to memorize and recite, and was frequently the one chosen to stand before the congregation and summarize the lesson. In this way, I became comfortable speaking in public, unfazed by the prospect of improvisation and fearless before a crowd. And when I was twelve, I was baptized in that church, according to its customs, first spending a week on the mourner's bench, and then standing in the baptismal font in the backyard of the church, all dressed in white, while Reverend Arrington, the old, authoritarian pastor who'd been in charge there for forty years, said, "Brother, I baptize you in the name of the Father, the Son, and the Holy Ghost." He dunked me then, from head to toe. The legend was that if you coughed or choked, you didn't have good religion and you'd have to do it again.

As memorable as that was, I wanted an authentic faith that was more than rote. As I became a teenager, I was passionate, ambitious, hungry, and yearning to find my place in the world. I wanted to know the living God. When I was about fourteen years old, a young man named Mike Moore became the coach of my baseball team. Mike had grown up in Number 8, but he wasn't like most of the other kids I knew. He was polite, good at sports, an excellent student, and notably the first person I ever met who planned to go away to college. Motivated, he carried the fresh air of the world with him and he had big dreams for his own future: after a conversion experience of his own, he became certain of his vocation to start a church and be a preacher, but not before spending a year in law school. Everybody liked Mike. I idolized him, wanted to be just like him.

Mike talked about Jesus all the time, and encouraged the baseball team to accompany him to Bible study. The Christianity he embraced and embodied was a vibrant faith, a contemporary Pentecostalism that started and ended with the importance of the Holy Spirit. Since its beginnings, in the first part of the twentieth century, Pentecostalism has always been about the Spirit, the third and most conceptually difficult aspect of the Christian Trinity, the breath of God that exists within all Christian believers. Those who have born-again experiences pay special tribute to the Spirit. They say it descends on them or infuses in them in that moment of conversion a kind of power that guides them, like a compass, toward holiness. Pentecostalism has its roots in the verses from the Book of Acts, which describes a crowd of Jesus's followers—one hundred twenty in all, including the disciples, women, Jesus's brothers—waiting for their resurrected Lord.

> *And suddenly there came a sound from heaven as of a rushing mighty wind, and it filled all the house where they were sitting. And there appeared unto them cloven tongues like as of fire, and it sat upon each of them. And they were all filled with the Holy Ghost, and began to speak with other tongues, as the Spirit gave them utterance.*

In Pentecostalism, the Spirit is potent, giving believers not just an ability to discern God's will for their lives but also often extraordinary, supernatural powers—an ability to speak in tongues and to heal the sick with the laying on of hands. The Pentecostalism that Mike taught assured me that you didn't have to be a cleaned-up version of yourself to earn these gifts or God's love. You didn't have to work up to anything, or gather points in heaven. You didn't have to quit smoking. You didn't have to quit drinking. You didn't have to come to a crisis point and resolve to change your ways. The whole point of God was that He loved you in your brokenness, that He didn't need you to be perfect. That was the miracle. That same understanding informs my approach with my patients. As they feel compelled to explain themselves, to rationalize their abortion decision, they often feel the need to invent a narrative that makes them appear virtuous, or that "cleans up" the details of their circumstances, in order to evoke my compassion. When I sense this, I tell them of my understanding (though I keep God out of it): Your need makes you worthy. You are fine the way you are.

Mike taught me that if I invited it to happen, I could be baptized in the Holy Spirit—and once I was, I could speak in tongues
and heal the sick and cast out demons, and more: that the Spirit
would lead me toward the most divine version of myself. "The
Spirit can pray for things you didn't know you needed to pray for,"
Mike told me. One Wednesday night, after baseball practice, Mike
took the whole team to Bible study. I was the only one who returned
again and again. I became one of those people you see with a Bible
always in his hand: reading, underlining, cross-referencing until I
knew the text by heart. I read not just Scripture, but commentaries
and interpretations of Scripture. Always a good student, this approach to religion appealed to my contemplative side.

On Sunday, May 14, 1978, when I was fifteen years old, I let
Jesus into my life and became born again. This was neither a sudden decision nor was it the kind of orgiastic event you hear about in
televangelists' accounts. I had no Technicolor visions. No sonorous,
disembodied voices from on high echoed in my ear or spoke to me
through the AM radio. I did not fall to the ground and weep. Mike
had instructed me, in fact, not to put too much store in emotional
experiences, which come and go. The Spirit, Mike said, is constant,
like a heartbeat. In Bible study, I had been reading about the life of
Paul, the former Jewish antagonist of the earliest Christians. Paul's
conversion—he was on the road to Damascus and saw a flash of light;
he heard the voice of Jesus, was blinded, and then, through a Christian
healer, was given sight again—initiated the first massive evangeliza-
tion effort. After his encounter with Jesus, Paul was inspired to greatness. He traveled ten thousand miles, according to legend, mostly on
foot but also by boat, to what is modern-day Israel, Syria, Greece, and
Turkey, preaching to the unconverted the truth of the gospel story. I

wanted that certainty and that greatness for my life. And I wanted that sense of divine guidance. Aware of the limitations my circumstances placed upon me, I was drawn to the idea that by giving myself over to God, I would have a new life. I would have a future and a plan.

It was the afternoon. Mike had told me that all I had to do to experience the love of the living God was to invite Him in. I wanted to try this, all by myself—without church, or a congregation or the peer pressure of an altar call, or the spectacle that can sometimes accompany such a moment. There was a red-dirt lot at the bottom of our hill, kitty-corner from my grandfather's hog pen, so dusty in the summer months that we would come away from our basketball games covered head to toe in grit, and it was so muddy when it rained that we couldn't make a ball bounce. Just beneath the basketball hoop at the edge of the lot was a large rock with a smooth surface. I sat myself down on the rock, all alone, with my Bible. The neighborhood was so still it seemed to be sleeping. I closed my eyes, and in the quiet of that afternoon I prayed for Jesus to come into my heart. And He did. And then I opened my eyes. Nothing was different— and yet, I was changed. It was still the same sunny day. The leaves on the trees were fluttering slightly. The familiar houses were there, in the same order, with the same front porches and screen doors, as they'd been my whole life. But I reckoned that I was different. There was somebody, something, inside of me, a spiritual resource to help me become my highest self. I had eternal life. And I had purpose. And now the task was to figure out what that purpose was.

. . .

God is love, and God does not judge, but God's people can become overly pious and haughty, and they can become inflexible. That's

what happened to me. My conversion impassioned and comforted
me, but it also made me both rigid and zealous. Mike and I went
door-to-door in Number 8, pressing tracts and pamphlets on anyone who answered, so insistent on our evangelism that some people
thought we had become Jehovah's Witnesses. We entered people's
houses and, certain of our own holiness, believed that our prayers
could exorcise evil spirits and restore the demonically possessed to
mental health. It was not uncommon among people of my mother's generation to believe in ghosts and spirits and evil spells—my
mother called it "putting roots" on someone—and I remember going
with Mike to the house of a woman named Marsha, at the request
of her family, to cast the demons out. Mike and I met Marsha in
her kitchen, and Mike began calling out to the devil we believed
inhabited her body. "Who are you, Marsha?" he commanded. "You
are not Marsha." I don't know if she was playing with him, but she
started looking around with crazy eyes and talking in a different
voice. Today, as a physician, I can say she was clearly in an altered
state—psychotic, depressed, or somewhere on the schizoaffective
spectrum. But back then, we didn't have Prozac, or Haldol. We had
Jesus, and we thought—we all thought—that through us Jesus would
ease Marsha's troubled mind.

My senior year of high school, Mike started his own church,
Faith Chapel, in the living room of his little house. That church had
eight or nine founding members, including myself; most of its origi-
nal members belonged to my own family—my brothers and sisters
converted to Jesus through me. (Now Mike Moore leads one of the
biggest mega-churches in Birmingham, with seven thousand members.) I was regarded as "gifted" with the Word: in my senior year
of high school, I was frequently invited to preach in church. That

spring, in 1981, I had been accepted to Mike's alma mater, Berea College, in Kentucky. I thought so highly of him, and we were so close, that I wanted to emulate him in everything. Berea was the only college to which I applied.

I was eighteen, and I was on top—or at least that's how I felt. The first in my family to head off to college, I was wrapping up loose ends at school, where I was finishing my term as the first black student-body president Ensley High School had ever elected. I had also been selected for a summer fellowship, one of eight or nine African American kids given summer jobs in science labs at the University of Alabama, Birmingham. My job was to help in the lab of Dr. Fred Feagin, a research physiologist who was developing a new mouthwash to prevent dental cavities and testing it on rhesus monkeys. I was given my first white coat, and a notebook in which to record the results of experiments—my first foray into the world of medical research, which built on my love for science as a subject in school. I loved to learn about how things worked. But at the same time, I held fast to my religion, wearing a lapel pin at all times that said JESUS and carrying around books like *How to Flow in the Super Supernatural* by John Osteen, the father of Joel. I thought I knew what God had called me to do, which was to use my voice and my oratorical gifts to preach His Word to anyone within the range of my voice. But I was also a scientist in training.

I wish I could say what follows doesn't pain me, but forty years later it still does. In April or May of that year, when I was so busy being important, I found out that my younger sister, Earnestine, was pregnant—at that point, probably three months along. She was fourteen years old and had entered puberty early. Her appearance was that of someone sixteen or seventeen years old. Unbeknownst to me, she had been seeing a friend of mine from the baseball team, a boy named Orlando Paulding, who was eighteen at the time. That winter, he had been coming around my grandfather's house a lot; I thought he had been coming to see me, but it was Earnestine he was really interested in. After she became pregnant, he stopped his visits, and in my ignorance and egotism I thought it had something to do with me. I didn't understand why our friendship had foundered.

One of my siblings told me the news. For months, my brothers and sisters had been trying to get together the money to help Earnestine pay for an abortion, but they were unsuccessful, as another family crisis took precedent. My brother Fred got arrested (over some unpaid parking tickets, or some such) and they had to use what little cash they had accumulated to pay for his bail. They hadn't asked me to help with the abortion fee, I think, because I was so explicitly a Christian and involved in Mike's church; they assumed that my very public role meant I wouldn't want to get involved.

Without the money to pay for an abortion, Earnestine continued with her pregnancy, and upon hearing of her situation, I did the most un-Christian thing imaginable. I judged her. I shut my little sister out. I was cold to her, indifferent, haughty. Even though we lived in the same house, I refused to speak to her that whole summer, and as she gained weight and became more noticeably pregnant, I refused to look her in the eye. The biblical literalism to which I adhered made me self-righteous with regard to the Christian ideal of sexual purity. I saw it in a formulaic way. Even as a teenage boy, I had the self-discipline to control my own sexual urges. Why couldn't she? It sounds harsh to say this, but I just thought my sister should have known better. I had seen other pregnant teenagers, and I knew that they were a fact of life. But in my spiritual immaturity—my thoughts had yet to evolve—I held Earnestine to a higher standard. "Good girls" didn't do this, and she was my sister.

Earnestine became "that girl," and I was no help or comfort to her at all. She drew disapproval from our neighbors, and, out of embarrassment and shame, she stopped going to church. The mothers of her closest friends instructed their daughters to stay away from her, while older boys, seeing her now as prey, began to constantly harass her with unwanted attention. It was my mother, finally, who showed Earnestine the compassion she deserved, doubly poignant to me now because I was almost as judgmental of my mother for openly having boyfriends and other sexual partners after her split from Daddy George. My mother's sexual activity was a humiliation to me. "Hold your head up," she told Earnestine. "You aren't the first person to be pregnant, and you won't be the last." Then she phoned Orlando and put him on the spot. "You going to help us with this baby?" she asked. And Orlando said he would.

In November 1981, Earnestine gave birth to a son. She named him Orlandis, and when I came home from college that year for Christmas, he was six weeks old. All at once, my disapproval melted away: everyone in the family called the baby "Fat," and when he grew into a boy, the nickname stuck. "Fat," we'd say, in echoes of our grandfather, "get me a soda, out of the fridge." Landis is now in his mid-thirties. A firefighter, he serves others and has a son of his own. And though Earnestine is divorced from his father, they had a good, long marriage and a second child nine years later.

The antis will hear this story and believe it supports their cause: prevented by circumstance from obtaining an abortion, a young girl with no resources raised a child. But I say that one example does not prove a rule. Bringing a child to adulthood is a gamble in the best of cases, and no individual ought to be forced into taking that risk if, after careful reflection, she decides the costs in this instance are too much to bear. The only person who can make this honest calculation is the woman herself, and once she has done so, must listen to the direction of her inner voice. No legislators or preachers can presume that they know better what she should do.

CHAPTER 4

Dreams

Sometimes, when you're in the midst of a thing, you can't see beyond your own circumstances. This is true for women contemplating the decision to terminate their pregnancies, and it was true for me as I matured and began to make consequential decisions about my own professional path. Thankfully, I had teachers and mentors from childhood through medical school and beyond who envisaged a bright future for me when I could not see it for myself. They never looked at my circumstances and made judgments about my abilities or my potential based on prejudicial ideas about what they, or their Bible or their parents or neighbors, thought I should become. I was a curious kid who loved to learn. They saw that. They saw my humanity. Time after time, people reached out to me to help lift me up or guide me out of circumstances that almost always predict a bleak future without prospects. These mentors are constantly in my mind as I engage with the women who come to me for care.

In the fall of 1981, I entered Berea College. Founded in 1855 by Reverend John G. Fee, a Christian minister who believed that white people and black people and men and women should be educated together, Berea had another advantage: it admitted promising students with limited resources from around the Appalachian region. No one at Berea has ever had to pay tuition; every student does some version of "work study." Based on a student's means, the school calculates a fee to cover room and board, and students are given jobs to help them work that off. Some semesters my fee was as little as $35. Sometimes it was as much as $300. Studying in a tiny, halcyon, financially accessible place with an excellent liberal arts program with fifteen hundred students, I felt like a pig in mud.

My junior year, I encountered another person who saw in me potential I didn't see in myself. Mike Moore saw my gifts for a deep Christian faith and for leadership and preaching. Dr. Thomas Beebe cultivated my love for science. Dr. Beebe was an eminence at Berea. A skinny white man in his sixties with a full beard and a passion for the outdoors, he had been the chairman of the chemistry department for decades. He always wore flannel shirts and hiking boots, even in class, appearing at all times as if he were just heading out to the Tetons for one of the camping trips he was famous for—taking a dozen students into the backcountry for a month of winter to rough it. To me, he looked like Grizzly Adams. Dr. Beebe taught Chemistry 1 and 2 and Organic Chemistry, and his reputation was legendary. I had excelled in science in high school, enough to win that summer job working with the rhesus monkeys. Religion had encouraged in me a sense of awe and wonder, but science helped me understand how things worked—the machinery beneath the mystery, which I'd loved ever since I played with beetles in my grandfather's yard. Beebe's courses were known to be terrifyingly difficult, and he didn't suffer fools. He counseled students who could not live up to his exacting standards to drop his course and find something else to do—and he famously went out of his way to help those in whom he saw potential.

My last years of high school and all the honors I had accrued during that time—as a National Honor Society member, as the first African American president of the student body, and as a first-string outfielder on the varsity baseball team—left me hopeful if not confident about my abilities to succeed in college. Academically, I thought I was ready. It didn't take long, however, to realize just how disillusioned I was. My first week there, I had taken a series of placement tests designed to gauge my ability in various subjects, and—though I had been in honors math at Ensley High—I was placed in remedial arithmetic, a class so basic that it was not listed as a college-level course and for which I received no credit. I discovered straight away that this elite culture, of test taking and strategic preparation for gateway exams, was entirely foreign to me. I didn't realize it at the time, but this is one of the known side-effects of systemic racism and class inequality: upon entering what others regard as "the real world," people raised in diminished environments can find it nearly impossible to thrive.

In my first two years of college, I didn't know to be strategic in my course selection, to choose courses in which I had the best chance to excel, thereby inflating my final transcript. Instead, I selected classes without too much regard with how they, or the grades I earned in them, would impact my future. As a result, my grade point average hovered at around 2.7. I didn't declare my major until my junior year, when I decided on biology with the goal of eventually becoming a high school biology teacher—literally the highest ambition I could imagine for myself. I enrolled in Dr. Beebe's class because Chemistry 1 was required. I was still close with Mike Moore, and the way I pictured it, I would return to Birmingham after college and teach during the day, while I helped Mike build his church, preaching and teaching the Word in my off hours. I approached Chemistry 1 with trepidation. Even before meeting him in person, Dr. Beebe's reputation inspired in me a healthy fear—what I would now call a positive stress. I entered his class scared, motivated, and wanting to do well.

Sometime during the first month of school, Dr. Beebe gave us a test on the periodic table, balancing chemical equations and chemical properties. Out of sixty-five students, only ten people passed. I was one of them. On the back of my test paper, Beebe had scrawled, "Strong work. It's clear that you understand the material. Come see me."

That afternoon, I made a pilgrimage to Dr. Beebe's office, a dark place that looked like a wizard's apothecary on the third floor of the science building, down a long hall and tucked into a corner. The labs all along the hallway looked like something out of Harry Potter: benches topped with big, overhanging hoods to capture smoke from explosions. On the walls hung cabinets filled with beakers and vials and jewel-colored chemicals and jars containing animal specimens and fetuses. In his office, Dr. Beebe was sitting at his big desk, facing a wall of floor-to-ceiling books, and he motioned for me to sit in a chair facing him. He asked me where I was from—he knew Alabama well—and what my aspirations were. As I talked, he listened, leaning back in his chair while he fiddled with a pen between his fingers and chewed on his lower lip. Then he got to the point.

"What do you plan to do for a career?"

"I thought about teaching biology," I said. I had probably never felt so shy.

"Have you ever considered going to medical school?"

The truth was, I never had. In the fifth grade, after I had done well on a state-mandated achievement test, a guidance counselor had sought me out and asked me what I liked to do. I told her I liked to work with my hands. She suggested that I consider becoming a carpenter, because back then carpenters were assured of earning seven dollars an hour. That seemed like a lot of money to me at the time, but even as a twelve-year-old I had the sense that the guidance counselor was selling me short. In the world that I came from, a teacher or a preacher was the best, the biggest, thing a kid might dream to be: professions that offered stability, fulfillment, social acceptability, an opportunity to be an example and a help to others, a steady income—and a path to some prominence. I wanted all of this. But medical school had never remotely been on my radar.

"I don't know if my grades are good enough," I said. "I don't know if I can be competitive." I told him my GPA, and my semester consigned to remedial math.

"Oh, you can be competitive," he said with confidence. Then, without ever using the words "affirmative action," Dr. Beebe told me that it wasn't a disadvantage to be a person of color. He seemed intent on making me aware that I was on a par with other students with similar backgrounds and experience, that there were pathways to success for me, and he would do everything in his power to help me navigate them. He suggested then and there that I take an MCAT prep course over the winter semester, and he helped me figure out how to take out a low-interest loan to pay for it. "We'll write you a recommendation," he said decisively, his face flushed and jolly as he stood up. The whole conversation took just twenty minutes, but I left his office feeling motivated, empowered. Perhaps this was what Jesus wanted me to do.

. . .

The idea took hold in my brain. I didn't personally know anyone who was a doctor. My main experience with doctors had been the emergency department pediatricians who had given me the epinephrine shots and curative doses of Coca-Cola when I was an asthmatic kid, and my only experience with African American doctors had been with two different Birmingham dentists. One of them grabbed two big, strong patients from the waiting room to help hold me down as he filled a cavity when I was about six years old. And the other was a smoker. I had gone to him for another filling when I was sixteen or seventeen, and, after he injected my gums with novocaine, he went outside for a cigarette as the anesthetic took effect. When he came back and put his fingers in my mouth, they tasted of nicotine, even though he had washed his hands.

It will sound silly to say this, but the only other major medical influence I had was the character of Doc Adams on the Western television show *Gunsmoke*. Doc could do anything—and he did, whenever he was called upon. He delivered babies, removed bullets, and treated dandruff. I liked this idea of doctoring: where every day presented different people and different problems to solve. That was the kind of doctor I wanted to be: helpful, calm in a crisis, competent in any situation. Medicine seemed to me, even more than teaching, to enable a person to embark on a path of lifelong learning, a place where I might consistently apply my curiosity with satisfying results, and where I might do good work with my hands. My mind hadn't yet made the connection between medicine and justice; that would happen later.

During Christmas break of my junior year, I went home and made an appointment with Dr. Henry Hoffman, the director of admissions at the medical school at the University of Alabama, Birmingham. Dr. Beebe had suggested that I do this, and I did. I'm not sure now how I worked up the nerve—if I was stupid, or brave, or a little bit of both, but I just called Dr. Hoffman's office and set up an informational interview. Then, on the designated day, I dressed in my best clothes: a light blue sweater, a fine polka-dot tie, and a pair of chinos I had gotten at Sears. As I drove downtown, the butterflies danced around in my stomach. UAB had the reputation of a good ol' boy school, and even during my high school internship, working on the development of a new mouthwash, I had never seen too many black doctors around the campus. It was hard to imagine myself in that role. But when I walked into Dr. Hoffman's office and he stood up from behind his giant, mahogany desk wearing a crisp, white lab coat, he extended his hand. He was so warm that I was immediately at ease.

"So you go to Berea," he said. "That's a good school."

I told Dr. Hoffman about how much I loved Berea; how intellectually stimulating the whole experience was for me. I told him about my favorite classes, Issues & Values and Chordate Morphology. I said I was a biology major, and I thought I wanted to be a doctor, but was worried that I didn't have the grades. My GPA was creeping northward, but it was still below 3.0.

Dr. Hoffman didn't seem the slightest bit concerned about my GPA. He liked that I was a local kid with big dreams, and he took a proprietary interest in me. The important thing, he told me, was to have an "ascending academic profile"—an incrementally increasing grade point average that demonstrated academic improvement even as the material grew ever more challenging. Then Dr. Hoffman gave me the gift of a lifetime: he suggested that I submit applications to summer programs for underrepresented students at Harvard and Tulane. These programs, he told me, helped pave the way for college-age medical school prospects from low-income and minority families by introducing them to top-notch professors, providing them with an elite-university transcript for summer coursework, and by teaching them strategies to help navigate the application process. Had I not met with Dr. Hoffman that day, I would never have known about these programs, never applied to them, and never found myself at Harvard the following summer. "Good luck to you," Dr. Hoffman said as I got up to leave. "I hope one day to see you in the applicant pool at UAB." I was so jazzed when I left his office, practically jumping out of my own skin.

All I had at that moment in my life were my dreams—a condition that made me exactly like every other twenty-year-old on earth. So many of the women who come to me are young—on the brink of their adult lives and filled with dreams. I think of myself at that moment in Dr. Hoffman's office, and of everything I wanted. And I think of Dr. Hoffman, Dr. Beebe, Mike Moore, my friends' parents in Wylam, and all the other older people in my life who told me it was right—appropriate, commendable—to want those things, even if those visions were in some way still flimsy and immature, built as they were on powerful adolescent imaginings and not as much on practical realities. And I wonder sometimes how supportive these teachers and mentors might have been had I presented myself to them as female and unintentionally pregnant. Would Dr. Beebe have so heartily encouraged me? Would Dr. Hoffman have sent me on my journey out of the South and into places where I would encounter people and ideas that I hadn't yet begun to conceive of? Or would they have failed to extend to a nineteen-year-old girl the same enthusiastic support that they did to me, feeling somehow that because of her biological ability to carry a fetus and give birth to a baby, her prospects and her limits were fundamentally different from mine, and that she might thus be obligated to cherish her dreams differently?

During a typical day in the abortion clinic, I see so many college students, as vulnerable as I was at that age, and as hungry. I'm thinking now of a woman who came to see me at the Montgomery clinic. Twenty-one years old, with a wiry build, she was a nationally ranked middle-distance runner. She lay back on the table, and as I administered the sonogram—she was ten weeks pregnant—she told me she had two questions. First, would an abortion impair her ability to have children? And second, how soon could she resume her training? She was trying to trim seconds off her eight-hundred-meter time in order to qualify for the Rio Olympics. But in the same breath she also said, almost in a whisper, "I feel so bad." She was certain she wanted to terminate her pregnancy, but she had been raised in the Catholic Church and felt the burden and the shame of betraying her faith. I see women in her state of mind all the time, shouldering the shame their culture places on them. If one in three American women have an abortion in their lifetimes, then some large proportion of those women have been raised in a religion or in a neighborhood that officially disapproves of their decision. As a Christian, I feel that it's my job to help offer a counternarrative: that God gave every woman gifts and the agency to realize those gifts, and that nothing about choosing to terminate a pregnancy or to delay childbearing puts a woman outside of God's love. I answered her questions truthfully. "No," I said, "an abortion won't impair your ability to have children. You can have children, as many as you want, at a time that works for you (assuming there are no underlying fertility issues that can't be treated). No, you can't run for a couple days," I told her, "but with your level of fitness, a couple days' rest won't hurt your speed. Better to recuperate properly and be perfectly healthy in the long term." Privately, my thoughts were these: *No God I believe in would judge this woman for wanting to be the best version of herself.* And so, though she hadn't asked me for anything else, I made my voice neutral and touched her knee. "Don't judge yourself," I said.

.   .   .

Harvard! I landed at Boston's Logan airport on a sunny day in June 1984, the summer the movie *Purple Rain* came out, before my senior year in college. I was twenty-one years old and had never been on an airplane before. I flew Delta from Lexington, Kentucky, and was seated in the last row of nonsmoking (which might as well have been the first row of smoking). All the cigarette smoke circulating within the confined quarters made me queasy, but I was out of my mind with excitement. The plane banked, and I got a view of the sparkling city: the Charles River and the redbrick quads and buildings beyond. Country mouse that I was, I paid twenty-five dollars for a fifteen-dollar cab ride to Harvard Square. Then I lugged my bags down toward the river, where I found my room in Mather House.

There were about ninety people enrolled in the Harvard Health Professions summer program, all underrepresented minority kids. We were African American, Latino, Native American, Pacific Islander. When everyone gathered in the dining hall that first evening, I remember feeling insecure, like everybody must have been more entitled to be there than I was. I came from little Berea College, with fifteen hundred students. But here were people from all over: Harvard; Boston University; University of California, Irvine; UCLA; Cornell; Washington University in St. Louis. Here I was, a young man from abject poverty, from a place where I had to walk four miles along the railroad tracks after baseball practice to get home. And now I was living in a residential hall named after the Puritan minister Increase Mather, in the place where you might say white privilege was born, a gateway to the best jobs and the most important people—if only you spoke the language, and knew the secret handshakes, and embraced the primacy of its culture. I remember feeling very much like a fraud.

It has been well established that minority students frequently founder on elite, white campuses. Finding themselves in an unfamiliar and hypercompetitive culture, they can get psyched out. And if the university isn't appropriately vigilant and supportive, it can enable their anxiety, turning fear of failure into failure itself, a self-fulfilling prophecy. In my case, insecurity was like a holy fear. Fighting back against my impostor syndrome, I became super engaged and motivated. I took two courses, one in microbiology called Infection, and a seminar in cardiovascular physiology. That summer I learned about hosts, vectors, and virulence, and about the Purkinje fibers of the heart. It soon became clear that Dr. Beebe had been right. Nothing about the material was beyond me. I understood it, and when we got together in the evenings in our study groups, I found myself explaining things to the people whom I initially imagined to be out of my league. By the end of the term I had an A– in cardiovascular physiology and a B+ in Infection, printed, for all the world to see, on a transcript with a Harvard seal.

But it wasn't just the Harvard imprimatur that gave me confidence. The Harvard program, designed as it was to help people exactly like me, doled out all kinds of strategic information that I might never have discovered on my own. Poor children are raised without so much more than material things. They are raised without a clear sense of their own horizons, but rather with a systematic suppression of possibility and a literal lack of access to pragmatic information about how successful people get things done. My assigned counselor, a rising second-year Harvard Medical School student, helped me write and rewrite the personal statement that would accompany my med school application until it was perfect. A Harvard admissions director told me about the American Medical College Application Service fee waiver, which enabled people with limited financial means to bypass the global application fees and apply to ten medical schools for free.

. . .

Poverty is an onerous burden, and not just because of how material need—not enough food, not enough income to cover the bills, no secure housing or easy access to sex education or birth control—afflicts individuals and families. People living in poverty are treated as second-class citizens in this country, deprived in a generalized way of the respect and compassion that should be accorded to every human being. I understood the broad and enduring impact of this diminishment on me much later when, as an adult, I flew home to Birmingham from Hawaii to sit by the bedside of Miss Lula Houston, an elderly woman who had been like a grandmother to me when I was a child. There I was, an MD, a professor, living in a place that most of the people in my neighborhood only fantasized about, coming home to a place that most of them never left. "Willie James, I'm sure glad you came to see me," Miss Lula said to me as I sat by her bedside. "Lord, Lord, Lord, I wish people could see you now. So many people said you were never going to be nothing." And I realized then that, even though I was considered smart and even though I was "a good boy," the people who loved me were betting against me because of the circumstances in which I was raised. Now that I have brought all that I was and all that I've learned back to the communities of my youth, I can truly relate to my patients: I understand how being poor and coming from a racially stigmatized group can threaten your sense of self-determination and agency. The women who come to me for abortions are choosing a path different from what others would script for them.

But the sharp lesson really came home to me much sooner than that, when I headed back to Birmingham after the Harvard program ended. I was staying at my grandfather's house, seeing family and old friends, and the day before I was to drive back to Berea to dive into my medical school applications, I came down with a raging case of strep throat. I lay home all day with muscle aches, fever, a sore throat, and a vile taste in my mouth, wondering how I would ever make the six-hour journey back to school. Finally, at around 9:00 p.m., I dragged myself into my used car and drove downtown to Cooper Green, the hospital for indigent people, and presented myself to the admitting nurses at the emergency department. With a high fever and an air of delirium, I must have looked pretty sick, but I was told I had to wait for the ear, nose, and throat doctor to arrive.

I sat there for seven hours, until about four thirty in the morning, when the ENT resident finally showed up, looking as if he had just stumbled out of bed. With a lamp on his head, he asked me to lean back while he stuck a long needle with a syringe on it into my tonsil to make sure I didn't have an abscess there. The needle didn't bother me—I wasn't squeamish—and was relieved when he gave me the all clear, writing a script for antibiotics and sending me home. But I was deeply offended by his lack of urgency—his indifference, and the indifference of the hospital staff, while I sat there for hours, waiting and waiting, feeling miserable all through the night. I felt, and I'm speculating here, that because this was a hospital for poor people who had no insurance, this doctor felt that our time had no value. He knew that there was a never-ending stream of poor people walking through his doors, and no matter how hard he worked, he would never clear his caseload. So he decided that he would sleep when he wanted, and that he would see me when he was ready. Perhaps it was my recent perspective, the glimpse I had gotten into the world of privilege, but my sense of wanting justice for people like me was piqued. As I rode back to school with a couple of buddies, curled up in my seat, still nursing my strep, I vowed that when I became a doctor, I would convey to my patients a sense of respect and value for their time—no matter how little money they had.

I followed the advice I'd gotten at Harvard and applied to medical schools in my home states of Alabama and Kentucky, as well as to some of the historically black university medical schools. I was accepted by almost all of them (including, to my great delight, the University of Alabama, by personal invitation from Dr. Hoffman). But I ended up at the University of Iowa because they agreed to carry my tuition bill and because they had a long history of sup-

porting minority students, proven by a double-digit minority en-
rollment. My first year of medical school, all my bills were paid,
due to the Scholarship for Students of Exceptional Financial Need,
a national grant. I was one of the twenty-four neediest first-year
medical students in the whole country—a dubious honor, to be sure.

Looking back now, I can see how fragile my dreams were, even
though they felt so real to me, and how dependent they were for survival on so many people who believed in them at least as much as I
did. There were wise people, who knew more than I did about the
world, who guided my future and helped me make the right choices
for myself. I worked hard and was directed toward special programs
designed to lift me and others like myself out of our circumstances
so that we might have a longer view. I was encouraged to nurture my
ambition, but was also pointed in the direction of real material help,
so that my ambition might bear fruit.

Perhaps most important, Mike Moore had taught me about the
radical nature of God's love—always possible, never punitive, and
never, ever conditional. I knew deep in my soul that I deserved to
become a doctor because I had the potential and drive to do so,
and that I was God's child, a situation that was not circumstantial.
And when I looked around me, I realized that not everyone—not
the guidance counselor in the fifth grade or the ENT attending at
Cooper Green—felt the same way about people who happened to be
less fortunate than they.

I say this with respect, but I think it's easy to misunderstand, or
to gloss over, what it means to be poor. Five hundred dollars, which
is approximately what a first-trimester surgical abortion costs, may
not seem like a lot of money to some people, but the facts of my
life help me to understand, at the level of my bones, just how much

it can be. There were semesters at Berea when I owed the school just a couple hundred dollars to pay for my room and board and couldn't find it because someone from home had called me up and needed a loan for something important and I couldn't say no. And I know with every pulse of my beating heart that I would never have found my way to medical school if the folks at Harvard hadn't told me about the application fee waiver, thus saving me fifteen hundred dollars, and if the folks at Iowa hadn't seen promise in me and offered me a tuition waiver on admission. There were structures in place, systems to help me realize my dreams.

The twenty-four-, forty-eight-, and seventy-two-hour waiting periods—the period of time between an initial visit to the clinic for counseling and the abortion appointment—enacted by twenty-seven states since 2010—have increased the burden on women who want to terminate their pregnancies by failing to provide them financial support. Every day, or week, a poor woman delays the procedure, the costs to her increase, not theoretically but in real terms—*and not having money is likely the main reason she wants an abortion in the first place.* In 2015, ThinkProgress, a website affiliated with the Center for American Progress, calculated the cost of an abortion to a woman living in a rural part of Wisconsin, if you factor in the gas, hotel, child-care expenses, and the lost hours of work necessary to abide by the state-mandated twenty-four-hour waiting period. The bill, including the cost of the first-trimester abortion itself, came to $1,380.

For a woman who doesn't want to be pregnant, government and establishment structures and systems do not open doors. They close them. They stand in her way, forcing her to pay more, not less, to claim her own future. As a young, poor, African American man with

an appetite for achievement, I was able to seize opportunities provided me—imperfect and scarce as they were—to become a doctor.
But for a young woman who happens to be unintentionally pregnant
and living in Alabama—or Mississippi or Texas or Indiana—there
are no such gateways. Worse. By enacting legislation that forces her
to wait, and by making it ever more difficult for abortion providers
to do their jobs safely and without trauma or risk to themselves, the
states are actively denying her future, and thus her humanity.

CHAPTER 5

Putting Her First

My decision to become an ob-gyn surprised even me. With Doc Adams as my mental model, I imagined a career as a folksy pillar of a small community, treating men and women, children and the elderly, for everything from poison ivy to late-stage cancer. Obstetrics and gynecology were never on my radar, and so I saved my ob-gyn rotation for the end of my medical school clerkship. It was, frankly, an afterthought. I didn't know any ob-gyns. I didn't have any aspirations in that direction. As far as the specialty went, I was uninitiated.

To my surprise, I fell completely in love. I fell for the content of the specialty, the physiology of women, the unpredictable routine. I loved the one-to-one contact with the patients, the fact that I could deploy my good hands and my technical skills in such a wide variety of settings: in prenatal care and labor and delivery as well as in oncology and gynecologic surgery. A woman might go through labor with ease, or she might need a cesarean section, and I loved that I had to be prepared and skilled to cope with either outcome. I loved the alternate perspective I gained on human physiology through learning about female anatomy and the endocrine system. And I loved that so many of the patients we saw were already healthy. These were, for the most part, not sick people. They were healthy people, doing what they could to keep themselves, their pregnancies, and their living children healthy as well.

In every ob-gyn department, the emphasis is on childbirth. Everything else—the treating of disease; the maintenance of menopause; reproductive health, including birth control and abortion care—is secondary. I remember with clarity one of the first times I ever witnessed childbirth. I had read about labor and delivery, of course, and had sat through lectures on the physiology of pregnancy; I knew the particulars of how a woman's body changes through the gestational stages of pregnancy, and how women are evolutionarily designed to accommodate those changes. But I had never seen it firsthand. One afternoon, as part of my rotation, I was scheduled to watch a woman give birth. As a third-year medical school student, I couldn't participate; my only role was to observe. My memory of a woman I'll call Mrs. Olson, however, is as clear as day. Mrs. Olson was from Waterloo, Iowa. She was Caucasian, her husband was African American, and she was admitted to labor and delivery in order to give birth to their third child. She was progressing swiftly, and panting as women do in the later stages of labor, but she didn't want to deliver until her husband was done parking the car. He hadn't been able to attend either of his previous children's births, and this was supposed to be the last one. "He better not miss it," she kept on saying. So as the baby was crowning, she refused to push, saying, "He better not miss it. He better not miss it." Nurses and other people were running around, looking for Mr. Olson, trying to get him upstairs, and just at that moment I came around the corner to get a better view and she looked up and saw me and yelled, "That's not him!"

Mr. Olson did make it in time. And he and I watched, in awe, as Mrs. Olson's vagina opened and she delivered an eight-pound baby girl. The labor and delivery staff cut the baby's umbilical cord and dried her off and suctioned out her airways. And then Mrs. Olson expelled the placenta, and her body shut down. I found it the most fascinating, and beautiful, process I had ever seen.

Ob-gyn felt like a good fit for me, the right fit. Partially, I think, this is because, as a fatherless child, I've always felt somewhat more at ease among women than I have among men, starting when, as a small child, I was a favorite of the neighborhood's wise women: teachers, librarians, and Sunday-school instructors—the recipient of so much kitchen table wit and wisdom. And partially it's because, in my maturity—though I wouldn't have put it this way as a medical student—I recognize in women's struggles reflections of my own. By choosing to care for women, I might spend my life helping a group of people stigmatized on the basis of appearance and circumstance, as I was; people who have to work diligently and against odds to build a sense of self and a reservoir of dignity. I didn't have an ideology of feminism at the time, nor the tools with which to measure oppression. Still, embedded in my choice to become an ob-gyn was the dawning sense that I wanted to spend a lifetime allied with women on the side of justice.

No one was more influential in my belief that a woman is entitled to make her own choices than my mother. My mother died on Sunday, September 3, 1989, during my fourth year of medical school, just as I was applying to residency programs. I usually spoke to her every Saturday morning, a holdover from the days when I was in high school and would wake early just to sit with her in the pre-dawn hours while biscuits were baking, and talk quietly before the rest of the house woke up. The previous Saturday we hadn't spoken. My youngest brother, Steve, answered the phone when I called and said she wasn't feeling well. I figured I'd talk to her later, and then I had a date, and work, and the day got away from me.

The person who phoned was my brother-in-law Orlando Pauld-ing, Earnestine's husband and the father of her child.

"Man," he said. "Your mom's gone."

I literally didn't understand what he had said.

"I'm sorry. Your mom. She just passed. She's passed."

I didn't faint, or wail. What I felt, instead, was like my heart fell out of my body and onto the floor. And if I could have ceased to live right then, I would have. It's not that I became suicidal. It's that I was not prepared to exist in the world without her in it. I called the attending doctors in charge of my rotation and gave them the news. I had to go to Birmingham and take care of arrangements. They told me to take as much time as I needed.

My mother had not been sick, but she was sickly. A lifelong smoker with hypertension, she was also an amputee. Since los-ing her leg she had become sedentary and gained a lot of weight. When Steve found her that Sunday morning, she was in her bed, not breathing—the same bed in the same room that used to be my grandfather's. Though the medical examiner left the "cause of death" space on her death certificate blank, my instincts and exper-tise tell me that she had a silent heart attack. She was just fifty-four years old.

I have felt pain, but never anything so deep. I flew home on Monday and went directly to the mortician, where I signed over the

check from a small burial policy she'd been paying into for years
to take care of the arrangements. The policy afforded her a basic,
no-frills casket. That night, and for the rest of that week, I slept in
my grandfather's house, the house that she was born in and died
in, by myself. All my siblings but Steve were living on their own at
the time. Steve, spooked, went to stay with Mary. That time alone
was therapeutic for me, for I was able to reflect on everything that
she had given me. My mother had a big and tender heart. She had a
deep sense of what was right and fair. She was faithful to God, and
even when she had no reason to be optimistic, she was optimistic.
I think, I hope, I have inherited these qualities from her, especially
an ability to keep things in perspective. Because I am a Christian, I
believe in heaven. When my mother crossed over to the next world,
she ceased to live separately from me. Now she lives with me, in the
beat of my heart.

The greatest gift she gave me was the ability to parent myself—a
fact I did not know but learned the hard way in the months after she
died as I struggled to make sense of my life without her in it. The
last time I had been home had been the previous May, on Mother's
Day, and it had been so meaningful to me to be able to give her a
hundred-dollar bill, which I had earned myself. "Don't tell anybody
you have this," I told her at the time. "Don't give it to anybody. Just
buy something for yourself." With her death, I grieved that I had lost
the opportunity to shower on her the creature comforts that she deserved. Long before I met Mike, or Dr. Beebe, or Dr. Hoffman, long
before I had ever heard of Harvard, my mother was the first person
who believed that a bright future awaited me. I longed to be able to
relieve the material deprivations under which she had suffered for
so long.

My mother's funeral was held at Faith Chapel Christian Center, her church home after I left for Berea. Mike Moore, my mentor, former pastor, and friend, presided, preaching a sermon titled "A Place Called Heaven." We paraded to the church through the streets of Number 8 from my grandfather's house, and I stood by her casket and had a good long cry. During the repast after the service, a strange and significant thing occurred. A family friend approached me and told me she knew who my biological father was: her uncle. Now that my mother was passed, did I want to be introduced? Every fatherless child holds fantasies of how different, how improved, life might be with the guiding influence of that absent parent, and though as a boy I never felt a deficit of parental love, I was curious. Once, when I was a child, I even worked up the nerve to ask my mother about my paternity, though this topic was off-limits. It took a lot of moxie for me to raise the subject.

"Who feeds you?" my mother asked me sharply in response.

"You do," I said, cowed.

"And who puts clothes on your back and pays the bills?"

"You do," I said.

"Then your father is who I say he is. I'm your momma and your daddy."

The way she put me in my place wounded me—I was a child—but that day at the church, at her funeral, I saw the many ways in which she had been right. My mother struggled mightily to provide for us; for all those years, she was both mother and father to us—and she loved us amply and well. I often say in jest that I had a daddy by committee: my friends' fathers were as attentive to me as they were to their own kin. Neither biology nor genetics had any bearing here. Through my childhood and adolescence, this man was not in my life. He gave my mother no help—financially, emotionally, or otherwise. He didn't teach me how to tie a tie, and he didn't buy me any books. As far as my mother was concerned, my paternity was her business, and at the age of twenty-seven, I was content to let her have the final word. I did not hesitate to give my friend an answer. I wasn't interested in meeting the man purported to have fathered me. And to honor any man with my acknowledgment of him felt to me an insult to the precious soul that we had buried. The day after my mother's funeral, I made arrangements to fly back to Iowa and go back to work. That was where I wanted to be.

CHAPTER 6

Practicing Abortion

I do not remember the first time I did an abortion. But there is one procedure I performed soon after my conversion in Hawaii that is seared into my memory. One of my regular ob-gyn patients, a woman I will call Rachel, had come to see me in my private practice in Honolulu. We were friendly. She and her husband were delightful, and I had delivered their two babies. Her older child, a son, would often accompany his mother to doctor visits. He was an extroverted kid, and as soon as he could talk, he would come over to me and ask to be picked up. He called me Uncle Parker, in the way that so many Hawaiian children address their elders—even though I'm sure his mother had instructed him to use the more formal "doctor." Rachel and her husband were eagerly expecting their third child, and at this particular prenatal visit I couldn't hear a fetal heartbeat. The pregnancy had failed to thrive. After confirming the diagnosis, I outlined for her three options: she could let the pregnancy pass spontaneously; I could give her medication to cause the uterus to empty; or I could perform what's known as a D&C: dilation and curettage, the surgical procedure done by a physician to extract a nonviable fetus from a woman's body. As a medical procedure, a D&C and an abortion are exactly the same. Even before my conversion on abortion, I had performed many, many of them—thousands, probably—but always in the operating room and always with the patient under a general anesthetic, fast asleep. In the university hospitals where I had worked, and by accepted practice at that time, general anesthesia for a D&C to treat miscarriage was the standard protocol. But by the time Rachel came to me, I had regularly been observing Dr. Kessel do abortions—outpatient procedures done with only a local anesthetic to numb the cervix—for months. I imagined that those hours of observation, plus my long years of experience treating miscarriages in the OR, gave me the skills I needed to do this very quick, very basic procedure in my office without the safety net of a general anesthetic. It still pains me to say that I was reassuring to her.

I didn't have the skills. Technically, everything went according to plan, but when I dilated Rachel's cervix, she felt more discomfort than either of us expected, and when I used the aspirator—the suction tube—to remove the products of conception, she felt a lot of cramping, and she cried out in pain. It was traumatic—as much for me as it was for her, I think, because I liked her so much and felt, deeply, that I had failed. This was not just any patient, but a woman whom I knew and liked, whose toddler called me Uncle. In the provision of necessary care, I had failed to make her comfortable during a procedure that should have been short and easy. It rattled me, for sure, and it was in that moment that my commitment to abortion care took another, deeper turn: I promised myself that my *willingness* to help must always be matched by my *ability* to help. I resigned my position as resident faculty at the University of

Hawaii and decided to go back into training—to learn as much as I could about abortion care so that I might never again find myself in this terrible position of feeling inept and causing undue pain. I am forever indebted to Rachel: she was bighearted and didn't hold my clumsiness against me; she continued to see me as her doctor the whole time I remained in Hawaii. It was she who validated for me what I already knew in theory: abortion is never totally painless. It is physically uncomfortable, sometimes painful. And because of this, it's doubly important that patients continue to have not just legal access to safe abortions, but practical access as well: doctors need to be trained in sufficient numbers to do abortions as quickly and painlessly as possible, while providing a maximum degree of compassion. Without that access, women will be driven to seek abortion from amateurs—or even to take matters into their own hands.

In the summer of 2006, I left Hawaii for an incredible opportunity. I moved to Ann Arbor, where I became the University of Michigan's first fellow in Family Planning, a professional development opportunity, very well funded by an anonymous donor and administered through the University of California, San Francisco. The fellowship gives doctors, even those mid-career, a chance to focus specifically on clinical abortion care and contraception, as well as to do classroom work in public health. There are about thirty such programs at universities around the country, a number that has been growing steadily since the fellowship was founded in 1991. In Michigan, I was the first person in this role, and I threw myself at the work, more determined than ever to acquire deep expertise in caring for the women few others wanted to care for. I knew no one there. I was forty-three years old. It was cold in Ann Arbor, and I was lonely. But my maturity gave me an advantage, and I approached my learning with a vigor and intentionality that were different from other phases of my education. Abortion care was what I wanted to do; an abortion provider was what I wanted to be. This was vocational training, and for two years I immersed myself in the art and science of caring for women in this way. It wasn't just the craft I wanted to learn—though it was that. It was the clinical work of dealing, in this intimate setting, with all the psychosocial issues that each woman has around abortion. I wanted to be present for every woman, no matter what her situation. So I would go to the local Planned Parenthood clinic and perform abortions, over and over, like the athlete who goes to the gym after practice to shoot three-pointers. Some days I saw fifteen women. Some days, thirty. However many patients showed up, I trained myself always to have the energy and concentration to see one more. I wanted to get to the point where the procedure was automatic, a synthesis of muscle memory and mental vigilance, allowing me to know instinctively both what was right and normal—in a woman who had uterine scarring from a cesarean section, in a woman with fibroids, in a woman who is obese—and how to react in a moment when something went wrong—how to avoid perforating the uterus and how to spot unusually heavy bleeding—the way an experienced driver swerves out of the way of an obstacle on the highway without becoming flustered or having to think consciously about what to do. I wanted to know how to handle a patient's anxiety, and her tears. I wanted to be so good, so incontrovertibly, undeniably expert at providing compassionate abortion care that no woman would ever have cause to suffer an ounce of additional anguish at my hands.

. . .

A legal abortion is the termination of a pregnancy before a fetus attains "viability," defined by the Supreme Court in 1973 in *Roe v. Wade* as the ability of a fetus to survive outside the womb with medical technical assistance. First-trimester surgical abortion, also known as "vacuum aspiration abortion," accounts for nearly 70 percent of all the abortions done in the United States. (Doctors frequently use the term D&C to mean the same thing: dilation and curettage technically involves manual scraping of the walls of the uterus with a long tool called a curette; it was the state of the art until the early 1970s when the suction technology became commonplace.) A vacuum aspiration abortion is a very simple, low-risk procedure that can be performed to terminate any pregnancy up to sixteen weeks. It is simpler than a colonoscopy or a tooth extraction. The risk of complications that result in hospitalizations is lower than 1 percent.

It's so safe that, when *Roe* passed, the expectation within the medical community was that regular ob-gyns would soon be providing abortions in their offices as routinely as any office-based procedure, but because of the inflamed politics around the issue, very few of them do. According to a 2011 study published by the journal *Obstetrics & Gynecology*, just 14 percent of ob-gyns perform abortions, although 97 percent say they've met with patients who want them. Ninety-four percent of the abortions performed in America are thus done in specialized clinics like the ones I work in—devoted specifically to this kind of care. About a third of these are done in Planned Parenthood clinics, which is the nation's largest abortion provider. The rest are performed in stand-alone clinics owned by individuals who operate them as small businesses.

Before obtaining a vacuum aspiration abortion, a woman must

have a urine test to confirm her pregnancy and a blood test to determine her blood type. The age of the fetus is measured forward from the last menstrual cycle, and *not*—as many people believe—from conception, because medicine is a rational science based on data: while you can empirically know when menstruation last occurred, you can't necessarily know which act of sexual intercourse resulted in this pregnancy. Mistakes in gestational dating happen all the time, especially with women who have irregular periods or who inconsistently use birth control. I explain these things here in this elementary way not to be condescending, but because in my years as an abortion provider I have found that many, many very well-educated women know surprisingly little about the way their own bodies work. In the Jackson Women's Health clinic in Mississippi, I once saw a twenty-one-year-old college student who presented herself to us when she was fifteen weeks and two days pregnant. She had no idea that she was that far along. She walked through our doors imagining that she was seven, or, at most, eight weeks.

Confusion like hers is very common. This woman was slightly obese, a health condition that frequently leads to an irregular menstrual cycle. Her sexual encounters were also sporadic—so when she started to feel nauseated and experienced some vomiting, she never imagined that she was pregnant and instead took herself to the college health clinic, where she was treated for a stomach virus. If she had waited four more days to call us, we would have had to turn her away. Mississippi has a twenty-four-hour waiting period, and a ban on abortion in outpatient clinics beyond sixteen gestational weeks. Together with all these bans and delays, limited health literacy can have perilous consequences. A woman who takes a while to under-

stand what's happening to her and then decides she wants to terminate her pregnancy can—literally—run out of time.

When they come in for their counseling, overwhelming numbers of women ask me if they can be put to sleep while they have
their procedure. It's understandable. They have usually heard that
the procedure can be painful, and their clarity around their abortion decision does not mean that they are free of anxiety about the
prospect of pain—or about their decision itself. (Think about the
number of women who choose epidurals during labor and birth:
they want the baby, but they want the drugs, too.) Usually, my answer to these women has to be no. Most stand-alone clinics are not
equipped to deliver general anesthesia, which carries its own set of
risks and restrictions, and the administering of which would only
inhibit access even more. In the Mississippi clinic where I worked
from 2012 to 2016 and in the clinic in Montgomery, Alabama, patients get no narcotics at all. Instead, they receive an antihistamine,
which causes some drowsiness, and a combination of Tylenol and
Motrin to dull the potent cramps that can occur as I empty the
uterus with the suction tube. At the West Alabama Women's Center
in Tuscaloosa, each patient gets an anxiolytic, like Xanax or Valium,
about half an hour before her procedure, as well as naproxen or ibu-
profen or some other over-the-counter pain relief. Since I started
working in Tuscaloosa, that clinic has also implemented the ability to administer moderate intravenous sedation, medicines such as
Versed or fentanyl—not so much that an anesthesiologist is required,
and not so much that a patient loses her gag reflex, or the ability to
protect her airway (one of the greatest risks in general anesthesia is
aspiration)—but enough to keep her a little less conscious. We fall
back on this option only in what we call "big" cases—such as when

someone is more than twenty weeks along and I believe the procedure can last more than fifteen minutes, or when an exam reveals
a very low threshold for pain. We used the IV sedation, for example, on a fourteen-year-old girl who came to us impregnated by her
mother's boyfriend. She knew for sure that she wanted an abortion,
but was so inconsolable and stressed out that she could not even
tolerate a pelvic exam—crying hysterically and paralyzed with fear.
But these are rare cases. Most of the time, women are surprised at
how fast the procedure goes and how relatively painless it is, even
without sedation, compared to their worst fears.

Although every abortion clinic sets its own "tone"—some feel
"homey," with art on the walls and dried flowers in vases on cre-
denzas, while others have a more modern, clinical aspect—every
abortion procedure room looks more or less the same. There's an
examining table outfitted with stirrups. A woman lies on it, un-
dressed from the waist down. In the presence of my assistant, she
follows my instruction to "scoot your bottom down to the end of
the table" and puts her feet above her hips into the stirrups so that
I can perform a bimanual exam to determine the position and size
of her uterus, and to make sure that she is experiencing no abnormal bleeding or infection. It is during this exam that I can tell
whether a woman's uterus is retroverted, and whether her cervix is
high or low, deep or tipped to the left or right. Knowing these things
helps me perform the procedure with more ease, for I can make
small decisions ahead of time, such as whether to grip her cervix
with a clamp at six o'clock, for a retroverted uterus, or at twelve
o'clock, for a normal one. After doing this check, and ensuring that
everything—hands, equipment, work area—is entirely sterile, I insert a speculum to hold the vagina open and shine a bright light into

the opening. "Cough," I say in a compassionate effort to mask the
needle prick, and when the patient does, I numb her cervix. This is
called a paracervical block, using usually 10–20 ccs of 1% lidocaine,
which takes effect instantaneously.

I then open the cervix with a series of dilators—thin plastic or
metal rods, the caliber of which increases in increments—until the
opening is as big as I need it to be, a measurement that correlates
directly to the gestational age of the fetus. At eight weeks, the cervix
needs to be open 8 mm. At sixteen weeks, it needs to be open 16 mm.
Then I insert a straw, called a cannula, through the opening and at-
tach that to a suction tube, which leads to a canister by my feet. I
flip a switch on the canister body, which turns on the vacuum, and,
with a circular motion, I sweep the walls of the uterus with the tube.
Within the space of a couple of minutes, the products of conception
are sucked through the tube and into the canister. When I withdraw
the cannula, the cervical opening closes somewhat, and the uterus
immediately begins to contract down to its normal size, a process
the patient perceives as cramps, which can be as intense as those
that can accompany menses, and last about four to five minutes.

While the patient heads to recovery, for crackers and juice and
to rest a while before she meets her ride home, I take the products
of conception back to the lab. (In some clinics, a lab tech will do this
work.) I place the small mass of tissue and blood into a fine-mesh
strainer that looks like something you'd find in an industrial kitchen,
and I run the whole thing for a minute under running water. Then
I transfer the contents of the strainer into a square plexiglass dish,
which I place on top of a light box. And there, I inspect what has just
come out of the woman's body: what I'm looking for is the fetal sac,
which, at a later gestational age, becomes the placenta, and, after

nine weeks, every one of the fetal parts—head, body, limbs—like a puzzle that has to be put back together. The fetal tissue has a fluffy, delicate aspect to it, whereas endometrial tissue, the uterine lining, is clumpier, more opaque, and spongy. I make sure I find every part, and I place them together, re-creating the fetus in the pan. I have done this so many times that it has become routine: no matter what these parts may look like, this is organic matter that does not add up to anything that can live on its own. This phase of the process is as crucial as any other, because it assures me that I've done my job completely and well. Abortion has an extremely low complication rate; when complications do occur, it's usually because a physician has left some piece of fetal tissue behind, a circumstance that can lead to a hospitalization for hemorrhage, infection, or both.

The procedure for disposing of these remains varies by state. The Mississippi clinic has a contract with a medical waste removal and disposal company. Once I've examined the remains, the lab techs carefully wrap the tissue in a sterile manner and turn it over to the contracting waste-removal firm, which disposes of it in accordance with the law. In Alabama, however, the state law requires a pathology report: our technicians send the products of conception to a lab that we, as do other clinics, have a contract with. There, technicians replicate the work I've just done, ensuring, once again, that the abortion is complete. The purpose of this corroborating exam is, in my opinion, another way in which the Alabama state legislature can hyperregulate me, and doctors like me, resulting in malpractice suits—and potentially shut us down. One verifiable case in which the state finds the fetal remains to be incomplete or far from the gestational age that we estimated, or one malpractice suit where the state can provide evidence supporting a plaintiff's claims, and we are sunk. This is why I always do a post-procedure ultrasound in Alabama: I take a photo of the woman's empty uterus after her abortion and keep it in her file—backup for me, in case anyone has a complaint, but more important as an additional measure to ensure that the process is complete.

The idea that abortion clinics might sell fetal tissue or "parts" for profit—as implied in the 2015 "sting" on Planned Parenthood, in which an anti-abortion group captured a Planned Parenthood official on video seeming to be discussing the prices for fetal parts, is both ludicrous and infuriating. I have worked in abortion clinics in eight states and for two years was the medical director of Planned Parenthood in the greater Washington, D.C., area. I can tell you, that doesn't happen. For one thing, most abortions—a full 91 percent of them—occur in the first trimester, when the fetus is no bigger, from crown to rump, than the first two digits of my pinkie finger. It can't be said to have any sizable, distinctive "parts" or organs at all. And although fetal tissue has been useful in medical research—sometimes extremely useful—it's just mischief-making to imply that there is a large, underground black market in fetal organs; it's nothing more than the work of antis hoping to layer more fear and anxiety around the business of abortion. The truth is this: No fetal material can be donated to research without the woman's explicit and signed consent. It is illegal to "sell" fetuses. Any fees collected by abortion clinics are transaction fees, covering the safe and sterile transport of tissue to a research facility—and most often those fees don't cover the costs of the job.

Still, anti-abortion forces are so focused on finding small vulnerabilities in the business of abortion care—any aspect of the procedure that can be restricted or legislated or impeded somehow—that the legal disposal of remains has become a focal point. In 2016, in order to stop abortion clinics from providing fetal material to research facilities, the state of Indiana passed a bill, signed into law by Governor Mike Pence, requiring all fetal remains to be treated like dead people and cremated or buried in accordance with the law—even if the woman who sought the abortion has no desire or wish for such a rite. These laws serve to perpetuate an atmosphere of suspicion and criminality around abortion, the sense that this legal health service is illicit, somehow. In Tuscaloosa, the health inspector can drop by the clinic unannounced at irregular intervals to inspect our Dumpsters and make sure we aren't throwing out any fetal material with the trash, as they have at times been obligated to do in the investigation of bogus reports called in by anti-abortion zealots.

I find that my patients are far more sensible, and far less histrionic, about the realities of this process than their elected representatives are. I once had a patient—a strong, light-skinned young woman with long, straight hair—who, after the procedure was over and the vacuum turned off, asked me if she could see the products of conception. The health aid in the room at the time, a protective, maternally minded woman, said no straight off; she was afraid the young woman, seeing what I see every day, would get too upset. But when I interrogated her interest, I found that she was rational, and curious. Like the women who want to keep their ultrasound pictures, she wanted to see with her own eyes what it was that she had chosen not to do. Having determined that her interest was neither morbid nor self-destructive, I led her, wearing socks and flip-flops and wrapped in her surgical blanket, down to the lab, where I showed her the strainer and the plexiglass dish. She looked at the fetal puzzle pieces for a moment. Expressionless, she said nothing. She looked into the dish as if she were taking a photo with her mind, and then she headed to recovery for crackers and juice.

. . .

Second-trimester abortions—in which the woman is more than sixteen but fewer than twenty-four weeks pregnant and the products of conception are not viable—are more complex to perform and more time-consuming. They require more specialized training. Because the fetuses in these cases veer toward the blurry line of "viability" as established in *Roe*, these are the procedures that have become the focus of so much anti-abortion political activism, and have been circumscribed by so much legislation. Since 2011, more than a dozen states have banned abortion weeks before the fetus becomes viable. In fact, when I was doing my abortion-care training in Ann Arbor, the abortion clinic where I worked performed procedures only up to twenty weeks—not because of any ban, but because the clinic itself wasn't equipped to do them. I was committed to developing expertise through twenty-four weeks, and so I did an immersion course at Planned Parenthood, Los Angeles, where late second-trimester abortions were performed in an outpatient setting, usually because the fetus carried a lethal anomaly and would not survive. These are among the most anguishing of cases, involving heartbroken couples usually receiving terrible news about wanted pregnancies. Contrary to the antis' portrayal of them, the doctors who perform these procedures are so far from heartless: they are compassionate health-care providers who have chosen a job in which they care for individuals at one of the most devastating crisis points of their lives.

Everything is more difficult in a second-trimester abortion. The

natural inclination of the cervix is to remain closed, especially in
the context of pregnancy, and it takes training and finesse to open
it safely and adequately to allow the extraction of a larger second-
trimester fetus. This can be achieved with the administration of
misoprostol, a drug primarily used for ulcer management that has
the useful side effect of softening the cervix, one to three hours before the procedure, or with osmotic dilators: Dilapan or laminaria—
toothpick-size sticks made of dried seaweed or synthetic materials
that expand to widen the cervical opening. Thus, a woman seeking a second-trimester abortion must spend most of a day, or even
overnight, waiting while her body becomes ready for the doctor to
perform the procedure. The numbing of the cervix and the dilation
proceeds in the same way as in a first-term procedure—but in a
second-trimester abortion I have to evacuate her uterus differently.
At sixteen weeks, the fetal skeleton is changing from soft cartilage
to bone, and the calvarium, or skull, is too ossified to be able to col-
lapse easily and fit through a tube. So I do the procedure manually,
with a process called dilation and evacuation, or D&E: a manual
"disarticulation" of the fetus itself, separating the fetus into smaller
parts using forceps, and pulling them, along with the placenta, out
of the uterus through the cervix, now widened to about 2.5 centime-
ters. Compared to a suction procedure, a D&E can take a relatively
long time, sometimes as much as fifteen minutes.

In these procedures, the risk of serious complications increases
(although at any gestational age the risk is less than 1 percent).
There's a higher chance of perforating the uterine wall with the forceps or doing damage to an adjacent organ, and a higher risk of
leaving some part of the pregnancy behind: part of the placenta can
get stuck on scar tissue from a caesarean, for example. The level of

skill and experience required of any physician doing these procedures is higher—and because these procedures are the focus of so
much legislative and activist attention—few doctors want to take
it on. There are only 1,700 active abortion providers in the United
States, and only about a third of them will do a procedure after
twenty weeks. In the South, there are fewer than ten doctors trained
and willing to do these procedures. The Tuscaloosa clinic where I
work is one of a few places in the South where a woman can get a
second-trimester abortion—and I am the only doctor in the area
willing to perform one. So while just about 9 percent of abortions
nationwide are performed beyond the first trimester, the proportion
is somewhat higher in Tuscaloosa.

I perform second-trimester abortions, within the legal limits of
state and federal law, because women tell me they need them. And
I outline the medical and scientific specifics of the procedure here,
because I believe that sentimentalizing, glossing over, or looking
away from medical facts about abortion is what allows reasonable
people to diminish in their minds the real stakes for women. People
frequently presume that a woman who has "let" her pregnancy drift
into the second trimester and then seeks an abortion must be care-
less or irresponsible. And sometimes she is, but things are not always what they appear. Often, a woman in this situation is dealing
with a much-wanted pregnancy, and discovers, rather late in the
game, that the fetus she's carrying has Potter syndrome, which pre-
vents lung development, or anencephaly, in which the fetus is missing parts of its skull and brain. These are anguishing circumstances
for women, and for couples, and I am glad to be able to provide this
service for them, as compassionately as I can.

More and more often, however, I see women in their second trimester because circumstance, and the constraining effects of new legislation, have forced them to delay their decision making until it's almost too late. Maybe a woman was forty-five years old and believed herself to be at the end of her fertility. Or maybe she was fourteen. Or maybe she knew she was pregnant early on, but she dawdled or was in denial or hoped that she and her boyfriend would reconcile. Or maybe her boyfriend was supportive and loving—up until the moment he found out she was pregnant or until the moment he started to beat her. Or maybe she did a lot of illegal drugs during the first trimester and had second thoughts about bringing that pregnancy to term. Or maybe it's nothing as dramatic as all that: maybe the logistics of her life, combined with poverty and the restrictive bans and waiting periods and lack of access, inhibited her ability to act with efficient haste. According to data from Planned Parenthood, more than a third of women having abortions in the second trimester said they delayed because they needed time to raise the money.

A young woman—in her twenties, with a couple of kids—came to see me in the Mississippi clinic. She thought she was about nine weeks pregnant, but when we did the sonogram we discovered that she was really more like thirteen weeks. This put her in a different price category. Mississippi has a twenty-four-hour waiting period, so if she could have scraped together the additional money, she would have come back the next day. But she did not. The next time I saw her was three weeks later, when I was back in Mississippi again. This time, when we did her sonogram, we calculated that the gestational age of the fetus she was carrying was at sixteen weeks plus one day. I had to tell her that, because she was over the line, I could not perform her abortion.

The woman started to beg. Please, she said to me. *Please.* I wanted to do her abortion. And I was incensed at the arbitrary turn her life had taken, due to the caprice and whim of several dozen legislators. She exceeded the ban by one day because she was poor. But I wouldn't perform her abortion. I couldn't. I live in a world where health department inspectors check my patient files and root around in my garbage cans. I could not risk breaking the law, even a law that I find unjust, to help one woman, and in so doing jeopardize my ability to help all women. The best I could do was to tell her about the Tuscaloosa clinic, which is a three-hour drive away. But she kept begging. She didn't know how she was going to get the extra money (as a pregnancy progresses, the cost of an abortion procedure rises) or how she was going to get to Tuscaloosa. I didn't tell her the thing that burned me most of all. If she lived in another place with less restrictive laws—Washington, D.C., for example—we could have seen her, done her counseling, and performed her abortion all on the very same day. She was penalized not just for being poor, but because she lived in the wrong zip code.

Delays, dead ends, and restrictions lead women to start feeling desperate. It should come as no surprise that the number of do-it-yourself abortions is on the rise. In March 2016, a *New York Times* op-ed writer and economist named Seth Stephens-Davidowitz used Google to demonstrate a correlation between women seeking information on DIY abortion and restrictive laws passed by states. He looked at search terms like "how to have a miscarriage" and "how to self-abort," and found some 700,000 such Google searches in 2015. Eight of the ten states with the highest search rates were also the states with the most restrictive laws. Mississippi, with only one abortion clinic, had the highest rate of searches for DIY abortion.

In Texas, where the number of abortion clinics has dropped from forty-one to seventeen between 2012 and 2015, surveys found that between 100,000 and 240,000 women had attempted a DIY abortion, either by illegally acquiring the abortion pill mifepristone or by taking the ulcer medicine misoprostol, which is easily available in Mexico—or by using herbs; homeopathic remedies; getting hit or punched in the abdomen; taking hormonal pills, alcohol, or illicit drugs; or experimenting with implements like coat hangers. It is not just the restrictive laws that account for this reversion to dark ages before *Roe*. It is the culture of shame and the hyped-up punitive political rhetoric that causes women, especially religiously observant women or women living in Bible Belt states where these laws are likeliest to be enacted, to desire a level of protection and privacy that prompts them to take matters into their own hands.

In 2016, I performed an abortion for a woman in Tuscaloosa who was sixteen weeks pregnant and had given birth twice by cesarean section. When I spoke to her, she indicated that she didn't have money to pay for the service and had decided, before seeking an abortion, to try a DIY method she'd found on the Internet. When she told me about it, I thought it sounded like a recipe for a salad. Following the instructions she found online, she went to the store and bought parsley and green mango. She ate the mango and the parsley leaves, and then placed the parsley stems deep into her vagina. Needless to say, it didn't work. I performed her abortion without a problem, but I was struck by the degree to which desperation can move one to do things that defy common sense and logic.

More telling, I once saw a woman in the Mississippi clinic, a white woman, about thirty-five years old, who was Christian and a nurse. She had taken a pill she had purchased online, advertised to cause miscarriage, and when it didn't work, she came to see me. She was very self-conscious and embarrassed about her accidental pregnancy and desperate that no one find out about her circumstances. She wasn't sure what she wanted to do—whether to continue with the pregnancy or go forward with the termination. What she wanted was reassurance from me that, if she decided to continue with the pregnancy, the pill she had ingested would do the fetus no harm. I told her I couldn't offer that. I had no idea what she had taken, and at seven weeks, the embryo would have been in the critical developmental stage. She left my office and never came back; I don't know what happened to her. Perhaps she gave birth to a healthy baby. Or perhaps she succeeded in self-terminating a second time. Or maybe she crossed state lines to have an abortion in a place where no one would recognize her. But her example raised a warning flag: it is extremely dangerous for anyone to take unidentifiable pills for any reason, and if one woman was brave enough to enter my office having pursued that course, then there are many others who are not. The proponents of the TRAP laws say they are looking after women's safety, but by forcing women into corners, both logistically and emotionally, the antis are creating an environment that is drastically unsafe. By making every woman's abortion decision into a very public political battle, they are jeopardizing women's health. Some women would rather take their chances and keep their privacy intact than deal with the psychoterrorism that can characterize the experience of entering an abortion clinic.

The easiest way for women to ensure privacy and discretion around their choice without endangering their health is "medication abortion," also known as "the abortion pill." This is mifepristone, known during its trial phase as RU 486. Approved by the FDA in 2000, it is effective up to ten weeks of pregnancy—essentially allowing a woman to have a pharmaceutically induced miscarriage at home. Mifepristone works to block progesterone receptors. Without progesterone, which tells the woman's body that she is pregnant, the uterine lining breaks down and the embryo cannot survive. The usual protocol in a medication abortion is this: a woman gets a dose of mifepristone from a doctor in an abortion clinic—or from her private doctor, if that doctor has registered with the manufacturer as an official provider. She is then sent home and instructed to insert four tabs of a second drug, misoprostol, between her cheek and gum approximately twenty-four hours later, two on each side. Misoprostol (which, as I mentioned, I also use in second-trimester abortions as a cervical preparation agent) is a common, inexpensive drug used for stomach maladies. It causes the cervix to soften and open. Together, the two medications cause the uterus to empty.

"Thirty minutes before you take the misoprostol, take some Advil to reduce the cramping," I advised a young woman at the Tuscaloosa clinic, a college student in pink sneakers who was six weeks along. "You should start bleeding within a few hours, and you may pass clots the size of an egg, or even a lemon. You can bleed heavily, soaking two pads an hour. That's normal. But if you bleed that heavily for more than two hours, call us." I always ask a woman who's had a medication abortion to come back to see me within a week or two for a follow-up visit.

Twenty percent of abortions in the United States are now medication abortions, and that number has been rising. Women like it because it allows them to terminate their pregnancies at home, at their convenience, in the evening when their kids are asleep, without having to miss work or find child care. (The clinic visit for medication abortions takes about ten minutes and there's no waiting around.) Some women say it feels "more natural." Many say it feels less invasive.

But with their TRAP laws, the antis are doing everything they can to block access to this type of abortion, too. Abortion rights activists envision a world in which women who live in a county with no abortion provider or who are barely able to keep up with their child-care and work responsibilities might get a consultation with a physician on Skype and then receive, remotely, a prescription for mifepristone. To block that access, the Alabama state legislature passed the Women's Health and Safety Act of 2013, which forbids the use of telemedicine to prescribe prescription drugs. The state of Mississippi has the same rule. Wide availability of mifepristone is the antis' worst nightmare, because it could allow women to terminate their pregnancies, in private, in consultation with their doctors, without ever having to enter an abortion clinic. If growing numbers of women continue to decide on medication abortions at home, then the antis will have nowhere to picket and no fences on which to hang their gruesome signs.

I am not the first person to say or think this, but having returned in my adulthood to make my home in the South, it is impossible not to think constantly about the analogy of the limits on women's reproductive rights to slavery. As an African American man descended from slaves and raised in the South, it is too easy for me to imagine what it's like to have no control over your body, your destiny, your life. Less than two hundred years ago, white men owned black people's bodies, and the southern legislatures that represented those white men's interests protected their right not just to buy and sell humans as they pleased but also to own the babies the black women carried, even before those babies were born. White men maintained jurisdiction over black women's bodies, in that they owned them and took possession of their babies. Insofar as abortion access is limited, this abuse of power extends to all women. I believe that the men who are passing the laws that limit medication abortion want to control women's bodies, which is not so far from wanting to own them outright.

. . .

Women who don't want a medication abortion or can't obtain one, whether because of bans and limits or because their pregnancy has progressed beyond the point where the pharmaceutical procedure is safe, turn to clinics where they have to entrust themselves to doctors like me. In my practice, establishing trust with the patient is at the core of what I do. If a patient has confidence in me, then I have the skills to get her through this procedure with minimum pain and anxiety so that she can get on with her life. In Michigan, I became highly skilled at the technique I call "verbicaine." This is a way of talking with patients in a direct, gentle, compassionate manner—about anything, really—to put them at ease. When women come to see me, they are resolved, they are empowered, and they have made a choice. Even so, they are frequently anxious, tearful, or on edge. I have found that verbicaine works at least as well as prescription medication. The more relaxed a woman is during her abortion, the less pain she feels and the easier it is for me to do my job well. And so I've developed what in another profession might be called patter—a rhythm of talking and questioning that starts the minute the woman enters the procedure room and I look into her eyes. Before I even put my hands on her, I talk to her about what is about to happen. I do not use a babying or condescending tone; I believe it's best to be gentle, but straightforward—to give her the respect of speaking to her adult to adult. There will be a pinch, I say, and maybe some discomfort, some cramping, the humming of the suction machine. These are the things that women can find unpleasant, and I say it the same way every time. Then, with one hand, I may touch one of her knees, tented under a blue cotton sheet. At the end of my explanation, I hold up my hand, fingers outspread and the palm facing toward her. Five minutes. In a first-trimester abortion, the whole procedure, from beginning to end, takes five minutes. This is usually reassuring, and I can see the anxiety in their eyes begin to dim. Most of these women already have children. They have been through labor and delivered a baby. They know they can stand anything for five minutes.

My next move is to talk, to try to figure out, in a fractional time span that to this patient may feel monumental or endless, who the woman is, what her interests are, how to reach her, in order to gain her trust. An abortion is, on a technical, medical level, a bodily invasion. Patients feel their vulnerability in a deep way, and this, coupled with the cultural shame, and whatever rumors or gossip they may have heard about the procedure, can make them incredibly agitated. Their bodies and muscles are as tense as can be, which makes it harder for me to do my job, harder for me to numb a cervix on a woman who is jumpy; harder for me to do the dilation procedure on a woman whose pelvic muscles are clenched tight. Women only truly relax when they feel that they have placed themselves in compassionate, expert hands, and when they see in my eyes and in my face and in my conversation that I have no judgment—none— about what they have decided to do. To gain a woman's trust, I try in short order to assess her character and her mood. Is she afraid? Is she looking to relieve stress by laughing? Where does she work? What are her dreams? In these conversations I can find myself talking about anything at all, from the fire-drill culture of emergency rooms, to my own childhood love for reading, especially Dr. Seuss, and particularly *Oh, the Places You'll Go!* Maybe we have geography in common. Where did this woman grow up? Where did she go to high school? Was it a rival school to mine? Did she run track? Play in the marching band? In Alabama, you can almost always talk about food—does she make corn bread with self-rising flour? Does she put ham hocks in her greens?—and if all else fails you can talk about football. Is she a fan of the Crimson Tide, the University of Alabama's national championship–winning football team? Or is she devoted to Auburn? In Alabama, everybody picks a side. Football here is a religion, and I can prove it. As a kid, I remember hearing a version of the Creation story that went like this: "And on the eighth day, God created the Alabama Crimson Tide!" Whole families have refused to join one another for Thanksgiving dinner, the rivalry is so fierce. The women in my waiting rooms are frequently wearing hats or hoodies pledging allegiance to one team or another.

And all the while, another part of my mind is simultaneously somewhere else. I think of my mind-set as a tightrope threaded between a meditative state, the way you feel when you are doing something you've done a million times, and a clinical hyperawareness, a readiness to deal with any challenge or anomaly that might present itself. I'm thinking about anatomy, hemostasis, integrity of the uterine scar, if present—anything that I might anticipate that allows me to operate slightly differently and avoid complication. As we chat about this and that, I punctuate my end of the conversation with relevant guidance and comfort, as needed. You're positioned right where I need you to be, I say. That's wonderful, perfect. Here's a little pinch. Relax. We're almost there. I may sing a few lines of a popular song, maybe get her to smile and tease me back, and by the time she figures out that I'm trying to distract her, it's over. "Is that it?" she asks. "You're done? You're sure?" Sure, I'm sure.

One thing people don't talk about enough is how happy so many women are to have had their abortions. No one wants to walk into an abortion clinic, to be sure, but many, many women are grateful and relieved when it's over. I remember a woman I saw in Montgomery, a radiology technician. She was in her thirties, pregnant with twins. We talked about our mutual love for books, and I told her that, with all the driving I do between abortion clinics, I frequently listen to books on tape. She told me about an old boyfriend who made her listen to an awful book on a long drive from the South to the North. She knew, listening to that book, that the relationship was ill-fated. We talked about how much she loved her job, the fast-paced nature of it, and about other places in the South that she had previously lived. She was totally relaxed throughout the whole thing, never winced: the verbicaine had worked. And when it was over, she said, "I know it's probably weird, but is there a way to get a copy of the ultrasound?"

"Oh, no," I said. "It's not weird. People want the pictures."

"You've been amazing," she said.

"Thank you." I smiled at her. "Can you say that again?" I asked, teasing her.

I am always reminded, in moments like this, that the bare medical facts of abortion—the bleeding, the pain, the cramping, the expulsion of material through the vaginal canal—are usually undertaken with so much equanimity by the women who seek them out. The women who are matter-of-fact, or stoic, as they undergo this procedure far outnumber those who are anxious or tearful. Women are used to blood—they see it every month—and most of them have been through labor. Most of the humans appalled by these visceral realities are the legislators who retain an unscientific squeamishness about female blood and physical discomfort. These happen to be, mostly, the males of the species.

CHAPTER 7

Slings and Arrows

On Sunday, May 31, 2009, I was just finishing up my final day as a teaching doctor in ob-gyn and family planning at Washington Hospital Center, in Washington, D.C., when text messages began flooding my cell phone. Dr. George Tiller, one of the abortion movement's bravest practitioners and an outspoken advocate for the rights of women—a man we in the abortion rights community sometimes called "St. George"—had been shot, point-blank, in the forehead.

Dr. Tiller was, as I am, a Christian, and at the moment of his assassination he had been standing in the vestibule of his home church, Reformation Lutheran, in Wichita, Kansas, handing out bulletins for the day's services. It was Pentecost—a joyous thanksgiving to God for the gift of the Holy Spirit—and the service had already commenced, with the choir singing an African song, and the senior pastor accompanying on drums. At a few minutes after ten in the morning, Scott Roeder, an anti-abortion extremist who used the online handle ServantofMessiah, entered the vestibule with a handgun, approached Dr. Tiller, and pulled the trigger. He then ran into the parking lot and threatened the churchgoers who happened to be lingering there, before fleeing the scene in a powder-blue Taurus. In the entrance to the church, one usher attempted CPR on Dr. Tiller, while another rushed into the sanctuary, found Jeanne Tiller, and escorted her down the aisle to the spot where her husband of forty-five years lay sprawled on his back in a pool of blood. Parishioners recollected later that they could hear her scream.

In 2006, as an eager first-year Family Planning fellow, I began attending meetings of the National Abortion Federation (or the NAF, as it is known), a professional association for abortion providers that establishes clinical standards of care, offers continuing education for practitioners, does clinic security assessments, and, through an anonymous donor, helps to subsidize abortion procedures and travel costs for poor women. At my very first meeting, I had been seated across the table from Dr. Tiller during an educational panel. His work and his bravery were legendary, and I was awestruck. He was one of three doctors in the country who continued to perform third-trimester abortions despite the vitriolic political outcry against the procedure and legislative attempts to criminalize doctors who performed them. He was a veteran, quite literally, of the abortion wars and wore his wounds with pride. His clinic, Women's Health Care Services, in Wichita, had been bombed twenty-three years earlier, and in 1993, a terrorist named Rachelle Shannon had shot Dr. Tiller in both his arms. In a gesture of defiance and outrage, Dr. Tiller had returned to the clinic the very next day, his arms bandaged from his wounds, and proceeded, as usual, to perform abortions. With fondness and reverence, abortion rights advocates regarded Dr. Tiller as more than a movement leader: he was a guru, a teacher, a saint. Even opponents, in awe of his toughness and righteousness, acknowledged that he was a warrior. But all his experience, and all the admiration in the world, couldn't keep him safe. So constantly bombarded was Dr. Tiller with threats on his life that he had been forced to turn his clinic into a fortress—bulletproof glass, floodlights, security cameras, and armed guards. It was hard to believe, as I regarded Dr. Tiller across a conference table that day in 2006, with his benign midwestern features and his cleft chin, that this mild person could be the object of so much fury. *This guy was shot for doing what you think you want to do!* I had thought to myself. *Are you sure about this?*

At the break, I approached him. "Dr. Tiller," I began, "I just want to let you know what a fan I am and how much—"

Tiller cut me off. "Hold on a second," he said. "Please call me George. There's no need to see yourself as any different. In this work, we are all the same, standing up for women and what we know to be right." To this day, I do not know exactly what he meant when he called me "different." Was Dr. Tiller referring to my relative inexperience—I was a newbie in this hardened crew—or to my race, and the fact that male African American abortion doctors are as rare as snow in July, or so I thought at the time. (In fact, there have always been black providers, working in the shadows, pre-*Roe*, to avoid the double stigma of race and abortion.) When I recall that conversation now, what I remember most is his generosity and his inclusiveness, the fact that he welcomed me as a fellow traveler, without even knowing my name. Over the years we became friendly, greeting each other at meetings, united as only comrades in the trenches can be, and in the Tuscaloosa clinic where I work, a letter from him hangs on the wall. "Abortion is a matter of the heart," it says. "For until one understands the heart of a woman, nothing else about abortion makes sense at all." Below it, his signature: *George Tiller.*

That Sunday, as my phone filled with messages and calls, my mood sank from exuberant to desolate—an emotional pivot I had not felt since twenty years earlier, upon receiving the news of the death of my mother. The sadness and loss I felt were deeply personal. But something even more powerful colored my grief as well. Instead of terror, or personal anxiety, I felt a hardening of my resolve, a refusal to be intimidated, and a tranquility, if I can call it that, about what I had come to see as my calling. Dr. Tiller's death made things simpler for me, and clearer: I would do what I knew to be right, and I would not succumb to fear.

At his trial, Scott Roeder pleaded not guilty on the basis of justifiable homicide. In his eyes, Tiller was a murderer. And in his opinion, Tiller deserved to die. A jury rejected that claim. Roeder was sentenced to life in prison with no chance of parole for fifty years. The jury saw Roeder, rightly, for what he was: a terrorist. He is also a fanatic. I have heard fanaticism defined as a doubling down of effort behind a misbegotten aim. If that is true, then conscientious resolve is fanaticism's antidote: a doubling down of effort behind a clear aim, despite the risk.

. . .

One of the things that infuriates me the most about the abortion wars, as they're called, is the way that the antis have shrouded their case in the language of God. With phrases like "pro-life" and "culture of life," the antis seized the moral high ground nearly forty years ago, and they retain it to this day, because abortion rights activists, the people who have been fighting for the rights of women, have never mounted a significant religious or moral counterargument. Never mind that every great justice cause, from abolition to same-sex marriage, has been waged in religious terms, in order to influence or inspire the souls of the passive or the undecided. Believing themselves too high-brow, or too rationalistic, or too scientifically minded to stoop to this level, pro-choice advocates have ignored the evidence and the history. Presuming that religion is a corrupting and divisive force, progressive and humanist people have failed to offer a moral, spiritual, ethical, or religious case for abortion rights and so have ceded those arguments to their opponents. Meanwhile, the tactics that the antis have used, for decades, have been so explicitly un-Christian (and I'm not just talking about the murder, arson, bombings, and other terrorist acts that have stained the anti-abortion movement since its inception) that it seems to me a wonder that any faithful Christian would want any part of them.

If you take anti-abortion rhetoric at face value, without knowing much about the Bible, you might assume that the antis have Scripture on their side. That's how dominant and pervasive their righteous rhetoric has become. But they do not. The Bible does not contain the word "abortion" anywhere in it. As an inspired document, the Bible is full of guidance for me about justice and love. But as a historical document, the Bible is a ruthless, unsparing record of the historic misogyny of the early Jewish and Christian people. The Bible was codified in centuries when women were only slightly more valuable than goats or sheep. Wives were property, bought and paid for with cash, like farm animals and household goods. Menstruation, the physiological event that occurs monthly in women of child-bearing age, was seen as defiling, a contamination: the Bible offers many rules concerning the separation of women from their com-

munities and families during their menstrual periods and the puri-
fication rituals required of them in the aftermath. The Bible offers
many picayune rules, similarly, about the conditions under which a
woman might have sex—which is, to say, never, except with her only
husband, who might have more than one wife—and the instances in
which she might be executed (stoned!) for violating these rules. In
the world of the Bible, bearing many children was a woman's most
important job; infertility was seen as a reason for everlasting shame
and humiliation—and even separation from God. Even in that ancient cultural context, however, abortion is never mentioned. The
only time the Hebrew Bible alludes to something like abortion is in
the Book of Exodus, which poses the following hypothetical: If two
men are fighting, and one man accidentally hurts the other man's
pregnant wife, and if as a result of that fracas the wife loses the
pregnancy, the aggressor must pay the husband a fine. (In the event
that the aggressor accidentally kills the man's wife, he then must
himself be killed.) The death of a fetus is regarded as a loss but not a
capital crime. Throughout Jewish scripture, a fetus becomes human
when—and only when—its head emerges from the birth canal. The
New Testament values marriage, sexual purity, and asceticism. But
it doesn't talk about abortion at all.

When I was growing up in fundamentalist churches in the
South, the subject of abortion was never preached from the pulpit.
Pastors preached fire-and-brimstone sermons against sexual pro-
miscuity and sexual infidelity. It was common, in the churches of
my childhood, to cast women in the role of temptress. As far back as
the Garden of Eden, the woman beguiled the man and led him into
the Fall, while the man—I remember finding this unfair, even as a
child—could abrogate his responsibility. *She tempted me*, the man

could say. *All I did was eat.* In the culture in which I grew up, this
was the underlying understanding, that because of their sexuality,
women had evil powers and were not very emotionally stable, and
the double standard was baked into our understanding of sex: any
person might fail to live up to God's expectations regarding purity
and fidelity, but the girls were the ones charged with guarding God's
line, and they were the ones punished when lust or dominance or
impatience or boredom were victorious.

Yet even though the religious culture in which I grew up was
misogynistic and regarded women's sexuality as shameful, abortion
was not something we concerned ourselves with. Until the 1980s,
abortion was seen as a political, legalistic issue and not a religious
one. Indeed, for most conservative churchgoers in the South, all
politics were seen as corrupting, desecrating influences. The Christian ideal was to separate from the world, to immerse oneself in the
Bible, and to leave politics to the heathens. This was true even in
many black churches during the civil rights movement. There were
many churches in Birmingham, but, given the number, not as many
of my neighbors as you would think participated in the civil rights
campaigns. In fact, people in the black community down south
frequently joke that if half the folks who claimed to have marched
with Dr. King had actually done so, the movement would have been
over a lot sooner! "Render therefore unto Caesar the things that are
Caesar's," my mother's friends said to one another, by which they
meant, keep your head down, mind your business, and let other
people worry about politics. Even when, as a teenager, I found
Jesus, the emphasis in the prosperity gospel I learned from Pastor Mike was on self-improvement and achievement—on the glories
and abundance made available to every individual through God.

All the churches and the church people I knew well were, like their conservative brothers and sisters throughout the nation, explicitly and intentionally apolitical.

In the years before *Roe*, Republicans—not Democrats—were the most outspoken advocates for abortion rights. Family planning and population control were Republican issues—rooted both in the small-government and individual-rights priorities of the right-wing establishment and also in some cases the more insidious attempts of white elites to curb reproduction among browner Americans. In 1970, New York's governor Nelson Rockefeller signed a bill legalizing abortion in New York. Two years later, his older brother, John D. Rockefeller III, working as an appointee of President Richard Nixon, called for improved access to contraception and liberalization of abortion laws. George Herbert Walker Bush was a long-standing supporter of Planned Parenthood, having sponsored and supported Title X, public funding of contraception for indigent women—right up until 1980, when he was being considered as vice president to run on the Republican ticket alongside Ronald Reagan. The right to safe and legal abortion appealed to Republicans because it went along with certain cherished conservative ideals: freedom from government intervention in personal decision making, and freedom to pursue the American Dream—giving each individual the opportunity to design his or her own future.

Not that I paid attention to any of this. I was a child. And then, as a teenager, I was knocking on doors, handing out tracts promising salvation through God. For Christians, the 1980 election changed everything. In the late seventies, a small but powerful alliance of Protestants, Catholics, and political strategists intent on putting Ronald Reagan in the White House came up with a cynical plan. By framing abortion as the most important threat in a broad secular assault on "family values"—and using rhetoric of the "sanctity of life" lifted directly from the Roman Catholic catechism—a group of what were essentially lobbyists found they could mobilize conservative voters throughout the Bible Belt, millions of citizens who had previously been politically passive and who regarded the polls as profane. The public face of this alliance was an organization called the Moral Majority, led by a fundamentalist Christian pastor from Virginia named Jerry Falwell, who conflated religion and politics by preaching that abortion was murder, and that the moral duty of a good and faithful Christian was to declare him- or herself to be "pro-life." It was, perhaps, the most successful marketing campaign ever launched in the political sphere, creating legions of single-issue voters who would stand in line at the polls in any weather to elect pro-life candidates.

Anti-abortion politics became, in an instant, part of a sweeping "traditional" worldview, focused, first and foremost, on overturning *Roe*. But it wasn't just *Roe*: the Moral Majority and their allies hated homosexuality, single parenthood, pornography, feminism, and legions of other secular ills. The antis reached back into their Bibles and discovered there "proof" for their anti-abortion beliefs, most notably a previously obscure verse from the Book of Jeremiah, which seemed to say "a person" existed in utero even before conception, even before the union of sperm and egg. *Before I formed you in the womb, I knew you; before you were born, I set you apart.* This understanding of conception is a religious understanding. But it was promulgated widely as secular truth.

Almost overnight, pulling the lever for the Republican candidate became the "Christian" way to signal a vote for "life," and for the way the God of the Bible said he wanted things to be. Millions of Christians flocked to the polls, electing Ronald Reagan in a landslide—their secondary (but no less explicit) motive to put a pro-life president in the White House who would appoint Supreme Court Justices who would overturn *Roe*. Women—and especially poor women, who disproportionately use abortion clinics—were the collateral damage of this political campaign, painted as heedless, heartless killers lacking in conscience, personal responsibility, and heart. "Abortion on demand now takes the lives of up to one and a half million unborn children a year," Ronald Reagan said in 1983 on the brink of being reelected, overwhelmingly, for a second term. "Human life legislation ending this tragedy will someday pass the Congress, and you and I must never rest until it does." And for the next dozen years, Republicans could count on mobilizing these conservative voters simply by raising the possibility that their "family values" were under attack.

Even in my most fundamentalist moments, this was no Christianity that I recognized as mine, starting with the fact that nearly every mother I knew was a single mother, including and most important my own, which argued for a broader definition of family values. More, the God I learned about from Pastor Mike was one of hope and transcendence—of pure joy. My God was ambitious for me. I knew for sure that He didn't care if I was poor, or black, or born into hardship. He didn't want me to be anything other than what I was, and He wanted to love me so that I would thrive and prosper, both materially and spiritually. At the time I admit I took the Word literally, in that I believed as a youth that, through Jesus, Mike could cast out demons and heal the sick, and I emulated the chastity of Jesus as much as I could. As a college student at Berea I embraced the rigidity of my Christian brothers and sisters, and held sexual purity up as the ultimate ideal. But even in college, I would have chafed against the absolutist views that the so-called religious right were promoting as Truth.

My inclination to feel on the "outside" of this sweeping conservative Christian movement had to do, of course, with the environment in which I was raised. The anti-abortion movement was launched and promulgated largely by whites, triggering in me a nausea and a primal loathing that I believe is the reasonable response of someone who grew up among folks who carried with them in their bodies memories of lynchings and the terrorism of the Ku Klux Klan. Many of my neighbors and relatives endured the real trauma of this violence, and I repudiated it viscerally. "My brother was cut up by white men and fed to the hogs," my grandfather used to tell me, "because no one ever found his body." The assaults on abortion clinics that started in the late seventies and continue to this day are nothing short of terrorist acts, targeting powerless people—women in need and the people who have decided in good conscience to help them—incited and enabled by the hateful language and culture that the antis have cultivated. There have been more than two hundred arson attacks and bombings of abortion clinics since the Supreme Court ruled in *Roe*. More than six hundred letters bogusly purporting to contain anthrax were sent to clinics between 1998 and 2002. Eleven people, including four doctors, have been assassinated for their affiliation with this work, which is legal. And most of these crimes were committed in the name of God.

In the early nineties, while I was still a medical resident buried in labor and delivery rooms in Cincinnati, Ohio, thousands of abortion protesters laid siege to all three abortion clinics in Wichita,

Kansas. Under the direction of a guerrilla anti-abortion outfit called Operation Rescue, in an initiative they called the Summer of Mercy, the protesters took particular aim at Dr. Tiller's clinic. Every day for six weeks, starting at seven in the morning, the protesters descended on Women's Health Care Services and would shout prayers, sing hymns, and yell at patients. "Don't murder your baby!" they would scream. Holding signs that said, BABIES KILLED HERE!, they would swarm the clinic doorways and then sit, for hours, reading Scripture aloud, barring any entrance or exit from the clinic itself. At one point, clinic staff were blockaded inside, unable to leave for thirty-six hours. Protesters chained themselves to the fence outside of Tiller's clinic, swooned, crawled, and lay on the ground. Police on horseback arrived to control the scene, and the protesters shimmied under the horses, forcing officers to drag them away. During the Wichita protest, two thousand seven hundred people were arrested and all three clinics in the city had to be temporarily closed.

The violence prompted by the Summer of Mercy led to new federal legislation, called the Freedom of Access to Clinic Entrances Act, which prohibits protesters from barring women from entering and leaving clinics. And it also led to ramped-up protection for patients and clinic workers, with abortion rights organizations enlisting thousands of orange-vested volunteers to escort women safely through clinic doors. These measures have helped, and the volume on clinic protests has quieted somewhat since its peak. But in my career as an abortion provider, I have worked in eleven clinics, and I have never, ever—not once—entered my workplace without being verbally assaulted and harassed by people who see it as their God-given role to interfere with me and my work, and to question my Christian faith and the judgment of my patients. I had my very

first experience doing a perp walk even before I was, in any official capacity, an abortion doctor. It was when I interviewed for the
reproductive-health fellowship at the University of Michigan. To
get to the administrative offices of the Planned Parenthood clinic
in Ann Arbor, I had to drive past protesters who lined the driveway, quietly holding signs that said, PLANNED PARENTHOOD KILLS BA-
BIES! This was a rude awakening, coming from Hawaii, one of the
first states in the country to legalize abortion. Because this behavior
was so foreign to me, I was more unsettled by these tame protesters
than I might have been. (I realized this later after I saw far worse.)
Once I took up residency in Ann Arbor, I drove past these protesters as a matter of course. Usually, I entered the clinic by the back
door, which provided me with more safety and security. Sometimes,
however, I entered by the front. This was safe for me, too, at the
time. For one thing, I was not yet visible in the reproductive-justice
movement. And for another, I am black. Due to the color of my skin,
none of the protesters lining the front walk ever assumed I was the
doctor who provided abortions. They assumed, instead, that I was
the irresponsible boyfriend who had gotten someone pregnant. I
would joke to my friends: "I'm never the doctor, just another 'baby
daddy'—a prolific one, since I'm at the clinic every week!" Worse:
the protesters assumed that I was probably forcing a woman to have
an abortion against her will. One of them once called through the
fence, "Sir! Sir! Don't make your wife kill your baby!"

Inside the clinics, we try, morbidly, to joke about our protesters. They are regulars and have become so familiar to us that we
know them by their first names; the earnest intensity with which
they carry out their mission—taking photos of everyone who enters and exits the clinic, including the kid who delivers the spicy

chicken wings in Montgomery—would be humorous if their stake-
outs weren't so rooted in hate and tinged with the implication of
violence. The person who owns and runs that clinic in Montgomery,
June Ayers, sets the tone by being fierce to the bone and, at the same
time, keeping her spirits light. Her staff and the patients benefit,
equally, from her natural generosity and warmth.

My policy, in general, is not to interact with protesters—not to
give them power by showing my fury. What would I gain? For eighteen months, I worked at Family Planning Associates in Chicago,
where there was a regular protester named Brian. He would show
up every day that I was on the schedule, sometimes as early as six
thirty in the morning, sometimes in the freezing, subzero weather.
He would stand outside the gate, smoking a cigarette in five feet of
snow, and when I walked to the clinic door from my car, he would
yell the same thing, every day. "You filthy Negro abortionist!" he'd
say. I'd usually keep my head down and try to avoid trouble, believing that these irrational protesters are not worth a minute of my
time or an ounce of my energy. But one day, my tolerance spent, I
walked up to Brian and looked him in the face.

"What is it about my reality that bothers you more?" I asked
him. "Is it that I'm a 'Negro,' as you call it? Or is it that I provide
abortions?"

"It's that you do abortions," he answered quickly.

"Then why refer to my race at all?"

"Oh," said Brian. "I just throw that in."

I had to laugh. Here was a man for whom there was one thing
worse than being black—and that was providing abortion care to
women who needed it.

I try, if I can, to see the humanity even in the people who hate me for what I do. At the Jackson Women's Health Organization, also known as the Pink House, there is a regular protester named Esther. Because we are in the South, even committed adversaries address each other formally and respectfully. In keeping with our southern gentility, we refer to her as "Miss Esther." She is an older white woman, slightly obese, with a thick Mississippi accent. She likes to yell at me through the wrought iron fence behind which she stands and advise me that I'm going to hell. I don't usually engage with her, but, again, one day I did. "I don't think you're interested in talking with me," I told her. "I think you're interested in talking *at* me." I told her what I believed, that Scripture does not forbid abortion. She told me I wasn't reading Scripture right.

"There is no 'right' interpretation of Scripture," I answered. Then Miss Esther said she hoped I didn't think she was being mean, and she prayed that I would one day start to practice "legitimate" medicine. I thanked her for her time.

. . .

Not every encounter is as civil. In the early months of February 2016, I received my first explicit death threat. It was lunchtime. I was eating takeout at my desk, not thinking about anything much. I had recently learned that people who were not your "friends" on Facebook could send you messages that would be cached in a separate folder, and I was browsing through that folder, just curious about who might have contacted me. And there, I found a message that was about three weeks old. "I know who you are," it said. "I know where you live. If you think killing babies is acceptable, you are DEAD wrong. You're on my radar now. I'll be watching you." The poster had obviously concocted a Facebook page expressly for the purpose of threatening my life, and I remember thinking, clear as day, *This is a death threat.* And then, my second thought: *Why am I not terrified?* I contacted Facebook and the chief of security at the National Abortion Federation, who contacted local law enforcement and the FBI. The incident was disconcerting, but I tried to shrug it off. That three weeks had transpired between the writing of the post and my finding it comforted me. So far, I have decided not to hire a security detail or to buy a bulletproof vest, feeling that if I get to the point where I'm more worried about my life than I am about the rights of women, I will stop doing abortions altogether.

The truth is that progress by abortion rights activists only stimulates the antis' taste for confrontation. One Sunday in June 2016, the very day before the Supreme Court ruled in favor of the Texas-based clinic Whole Woman's Health, asserting that by restricting access to abortion clinics, the TRAP laws passed by the state of Texas constituted an "undue burden" on women seeking legal abortion care, a group of picketers showed up to "pray," as they call it, at the front door of my home in Birmingham. I do not know how they got my address. Fortunately, I was not at home that day. In anticipation of the court's decision, I was already on my way to Washington, D.C. But in front of my home, on the quiet city block where I live, with a progressive church just down the street and a four-star restaurant in pitching distance, the antis set up camp and stayed there all day. They counted rosaries and got on their knees. And they held posters aloft. One of them said, WILLIE PARKER DOES THIS TO CHILDREN, before a photoshopped, bloody image of a disarticulated fetus that looked like carnage from a war movie.

Everybody who loves me worries about my safety "all the time," as my youngest brother, Steve, puts it. Earnestine always wants a text from me when I'm traveling, constant assurance that I'm safe and sound. Many others—friends, lovers, employers, colleagues— have begged me to take more aggressive safety precautions, and it is a deep frustration to them that I refuse. I don't take their concern lightly, but I believe you don't negotiate with terrorists; you don't give in to fear. Instead, I deflect their concern with a joke: I don't need a vest, I say. My best protection is my everyday self. I can walk around in plain sight because no one on earth expects a large, bald black man in sweats and a baseball cap to be a doctor at all, let alone one of the last abortion doctors in the South. But the serious answer to their concern is this: I've right-sized the risk in my mind. I try to confront real risk, and deal with that, and not the hypothetical risk. I take what reasonable precautions I can without upending my life. I never give my mailing address or my e-mail to strangers. And when I arrive at work, I park my car in a different space each time: it seems prudent not to advertise the make and model of my car.

There's another, philosophical element to my risk-benefit analysis. All my lifelong heroes have been accosted, or beaten, or assaulted for their righteous stands on human rights, specifically civil rights, and I see the work my peers and I do as similar to theirs. When the work you do is threatening, revolutionary, or life-altering for people, there's really no point, for me at least, in being clandestine about it. I understood that in undertaking this work, I would be in the public eye and therefore in harm's way, and so before I started performing abortions full-time, I considered all the risks, even the hypothetical ones, in order to gain a psychic comfort level: I might get shot at, accosted at the lunch counter, or threatened on the phone, or have my house burned or my car bombed. Having turned each one of these possibilities over carefully in my mind,

I was able to find a space of tranquility. The fact is, you might wake up one morning and get electrocuted by your coffee grinder. You might get hit by a bus while crossing the street. There's risk with everything, and it's a given that we're all going to die. As the gospel says, "No one knows the day or the hour." So the only thing about which you have any choice is how you will live. And I've chosen to live according to my principles and by trying to make a difference. I don't equivocate at all on the importance of the work I do being an abortion provider. And that leaves me very satisfied.

Dr. King said it. And Malcolm X said it. There are fates worse than death. A life with no purpose would for me not be a life worth living. I have no desire to die prematurely, but I am more intent on avoiding a death of spirit than I am avoiding harm for my decision to respect women and honor women, to help them achieve their goals and preserve their dignity.

At the same time, I'm only human. So even though I'm confident about my calling—I'm right with myself, morally, and I have adjusted to living under a unique kind of stress—I experience an involuntary shiver each morning when I arrive at work, turn off the key, and glimpse David or Brian or Doug, three different men defending the same patriarchal system in three different states, across the parking lot and see the bloody posters and the telephoto lenses, and hear harsh white male voices bellowing at me. I have been told that I come across as cool, even monkish in my demeanor, but I am not a martyr or a saint. The bare-bones truth is that I am outraged on a daily basis that I have to live with this threat, that the implication of violence has been normalized. Even more outrageous to me is that the women I serve face threats far worse than this.

The threat of violence surrounding the practice of abortion care is so relentless and so unnerving that even well-meaning doctors are persuaded not to undertake the risk. One of my colleagues, a doctor named Diane Horvath-Cosper, a young physician and new mother who works as an abortion provider in Washington, D.C., was shocked to find on an anti-abortion website a photograph of herself and her one-year-old daughter with a clear message that implied she was being watched by anti-abortion forces. And when she began to speak out about abortion rights, and the dangers that abortion providers face, her bosses forbade her from doing so—they did not want to draw additional, undue attention to their hospital's abortion practice. So Diane, who is brave and committed, filed a civil rights complaint and called Physicians for Reproductive Health, a physician-led advocacy organization whose board I now chair, to see if they might help her get some support and guidance, and now she regularly speaks out about the anti-abortion activists who made implied threats against her one-year-old child. But Dr. Horvath-Cosper is the exception, not the rule. More physicians retreat from this stress than embrace it.

Increasingly, ob-gyn residency programs in the United States are beginning to offer abortion care as a component of graduate medical education. Of the residents who are trained, the vast majority choose not to perform abortions as a matter of course—preferring to refer their patients to someone like me rather than live in the shadow of constant unpleasantness and risk. The terrorism of the antis in the name of Christ has thus had the desired effect. Decades of shootings and bombings and shouting and protesting has meant that the number of doctors willing to perform abortions has dwindled. In 1981 there were 2,900 abortion providers and only 1,720 in 2011, a 41 percent decline, and the number of doctors willing to admit that they do abortions is even smaller. This is the state of things, even though the American College of Obstetricians and Gynecologists, the professional organization representing us, supports access to safe abortion, and the overwhelming number of ob-gyns are pro-choice.

. . .

The truth is, no one wants their kids to go to school or church and be taunted and called names for the work they do. My friend Gloria Gray, who owns and runs the abortion clinic in Tuscaloosa, Alabama, was raised in the church—"You didn't go anywhere if you didn't go to church," she told me—and finds that as she has gotten older, her world has grown increasingly small: few of her old friends and neighbors speak to her anymore. Very few people want to live as I do, a bachelor, a vagrant—a conscious choice that I have made in order not to bear the responsibility of putting others in harm's way. I chose not to buy the house next door to my brother Fred when it became available—because what if his house burned when they bombed mine? Or what if a so-called Christian with a gun mistook him for me? He is taller than I am, but in many ways we look the same.

We know, from experience during the dark ages before *Roe*, that women intent on terminating their pregnancies will find a way. According to the Guttmacher Institute, there were more than a million self-induced and illegal abortions a year during the fifties and sixties—approximately the same number of legal abortions as the present day. But death and injury rates were much, much higher. Complications from abortion was listed as the official cause of death for 2,700 women in 1930, a number that is likely to be conservative, since many physicians and coroners lied to protect the reputations of family members. In addition, many women received ghastly injuries from self-inflicted or amateurish abortions. Coat hangers, knitting needles, or bicycle pumps were inserted into their uteri, resulting in puncture wounds, hemorrhages, infections, and embolism. The rate of death from illegal abortion decreased in the decades pre-*Roe*—not because fewer women were seeking to terminate their pregnancies, but because of the widespread use of effective antibiotics. Women will seek abortion whether it's safe and legal or not—even at the risk of their own lives.

As legitimate abortion doctors are impelled to hide, and top-notch physicians are dissuaded from undertaking this work, the number of quacks and predators will increase. In 2010, the FBI raided the West Philadelphia abortion clinic of a doctor named Kermit Gosnell, whose illegal practices and unsanitary facilities led to innumerable hospitalizations as well as to the death of one woman, named Karnamaya Mongar, who received an overdose of an opioid analgesic. The conditions the FBI found in Gosnell's clinic were appalling. There were blood and urine stains everywhere, and semiconscious patients lay on dirty recliners under bloody blankets. A flea-ridden cat roamed the clinic freely, leaving feces on the floor. Fetal remains were stored in milk jugs and cat food containers. According to testimony at his trial, Gosnell regularly performed abortions after twenty-four weeks, beyond the legal limit in Pennsylvania, and his employees told authorities that babies born alive had been killed when Gosnell snipped their spinal cords with a pair of scissors.

Gosnell charged 25 to 40 percent less than the Planned Parenthood clinic less than three miles away, and some of the women who sought his care did so, they said, because they had nowhere else to go. They either could not afford the $500 fee that their Medicaid would not pay (thanks to the Hyde Amendment), or they had delayed their decision until it was too late, and Gosnell would do abortions at any stage. Gosnell made himself indispensable because he was the last, awful resort for young girls who couldn't get permission from their parents and for people too poor to pay a legitimate doctor. At age seventy-two, Gosnell received a life sentence without a possibility of parole.

Gosnell is what happens when abortion becomes too difficult to procure, and when the occupation itself—abortion provider—is something too socially disreputable for any young, idealistic doctor to undertake. There is no excuse for Kermit Gosnell, who was a criminal and an inhumane predator of women. But he is a boon to the anti-abortion forces, because his heinous misdeeds tarnish all of us who do take this work seriously and do it skillfully and well.

Doctors like Gosnell are able to emerge because the culture of intimidation scares the good, brave physicians away. In the aftermath of Dr. Tiller's death, abortion providers collectively got very, very nervous. They were forced, very reasonably, to search their souls—for in the face of that cold-blooded murder, the risk they undertook every day was revealed incontrovertible. *Is it worth it?* people wondered. *Do I dare to continue?* The community of abortion providers, usually very tight-knit, grew silent, and I became concerned that the silence was enabling an echo chamber of fear. So, in an effort to calm and encourage my colleagues, hoping to share with them the soul lesson I had received from the story of the Good Samaritan and some of the tranquility I felt, I posted a letter on a LISTSERV of the Family Planning Fellowship. Fear and courage "are often framed as polar opposites, but in fact I experience them as complimentary," I wrote. Fear—the fear of the priest and the Levite—is rational, healthy, and self-preserving. Courage, on the other hand, "has to be chosen and taken. We often take the fear and leave the courage, when we should do the converse: leave the fear and take the courage." Seeking to console, I shared with my colleagues an e-mail Dr. Tiller himself had written and distributed widely some eight years before.

He wrote: "Being involved in a philosophical Armageddon, such as slavery or abortion, adds dimension to one's existence, crystallizes the vital priorities, and adds clarity to the purpose of being. The idea is to be in the purpose and neither live entirely for the purpose or die daily for the purpose."

In my note to my colleagues, I called on my spiritual mentor, Dr. King, to help me magnify Tiller's own words. Harm to anyone you know on the basis of the thing you hold in common is reason for pause, I explained. But for me, Dr. Tiller's execution served as a stand-up call, not a wake-up call. When Dr. King alluded to death threats during the Montgomery bus boycott, he described incessant calls to his home. "Nigger," one of the callers said, "we are tired of you and your mess now. And if you aren't out of town in three days, we're going to blow your brains out and blow up your house!" Dr. King had a newborn baby at home in those days, and he recalled that, in the moment of crisis, the voice of God was as audible for him as it ever was. It said, "Stand up for righteousness, stand up for justice, stand up for truth. And lo I will be with you, even unto the end of the world." That response seemed relevant in the fight before us.

I'll never know what those who disagreed with me think. They didn't share their responses. But I do know that I received many personal expressions of thanks to my missive. Fellow providers told me, in private, that they were less afraid and less intimidated after I put the incident into perspective for them. More, I think the fellowship of brave—there is no other way to describe them—abortion providers simply appreciated my articulation of the calculus we must take into account. The question all of us faced after Dr. Tiller's death was this: How do we move forward now, understanding that the risk of death is real? It must be the same feeling that soldiers have as they go into battle. They know that in the conflict people will die, and that by going on the front lines the risk is direct. How do you put that into perspective? I was able to speak the truth in a way that did not defy logic, but instead put fear in its place. Fear is a rational response to such an event, and looked at that way, as the other side of courage, it can be empowering.

In recent years, a new generation of physicians and other health-care providers has stepped forward, people who prioritize abortion access and training above their concerns about safety and risk. Not so long ago, the only doctors who provided abortions were the ones who lived through the years pre-*Roe* and saw firsthand the disastrous consequences of illegal abortion. As a result, the abortion doctors were an aging breed, and no one was stepping in to replace them. Fortunately, this is changing. Thanks to the same Family Planning Fellowship under which I trained, there are now literally hundreds of doctors with the expertise to do surgical abortion up to twenty-four weeks. Also, the Ryan Program, named in honor of the noted gynecologist and medical educator Dr. Kenneth Ryan and launched at the University of California, San Francisco, in 1999, provides funds and support to any ob-gyn residency program that wants to incorporate abortion care in its regular training—with the goal of making abortion an integrated part of women's health and not a separate professional track. In 1993, the American College of Obstetrics and Physicians changed its guidelines and reaffirmed its position to consider abortion a core competency in women's health; as a consequence, medical students are beginning to insist that the ob-gyn residencies to which they apply offer abortion training. Family practice doctors, nurse practitioners, nurses—all are beginning to demand that abortion training be more widely available to them and not contained only within the ob-gyn specialty. All these are efforts to normalize and destigmatize the practice of abortion care so that being a person who provides abortions is as unremarkable as any professional choice.

CHAPTER 8

Preaching Truth

In 2006, while I was still in Michigan, I was tapped by the National Abortion Federation to help write a letter protesting the Hyde Amendment and recommending that it be overturned by executive order. Contrary to popular belief, the Hyde Amendment is not a federal law. It is a "rider," attached to every appropriations bill since 1976, that prohibits the use of federal money for abortion except in cases of rape or incest or to save the life of the mother. Its impact is clear. And it is brutally discriminatory. The Hyde Amendment bars poor women from using Medicaid, their government-funded health insurance, to pay for abortion. In this way, it targets America's most vulnerable citizens—the one in five women of reproductive age who live in poverty—by forcing them either to find cash they don't have in order to terminate a pregnancy or to raise children they don't want or can't provide for.

In Michigan, I was beginning to understand how my clinical experience with patients might inform and enhance a life of advocacy; the best advocacy is always storytelling. The truth of people's lives is what moves hearts. And so, as I helped NAF craft this letter, I considered the injustice of Hyde through my clinical experience.

In the same month at the University of Michigan hospital, I saw two patients, both recipients of Medicaid, both living below the poverty line. The first was a thirty-seven-year-old African American woman with AIDS. Her disease had put her into renal and liver failure. And yet she was still healthy enough to become pregnant. When I saw her, she was fifteen weeks along, with two young children at home. She wanted an abortion, and her doctors agreed that an abortion was a medically indicated necessity; they thought the fragility of her organs would not allow her to survive a pregnancy. The second case was a white woman, thirty-two years old, an IV drug user with a history of heart-valve replacement surgeries. When I saw her, she was still in her first trimester, and her valve was leaking, which compromised her cardiovascular health. She wanted an abortion and her doctors agreed, believing that her weak heart could not support the extra cardiovascular work of maintaining a pregnancy; we thought that bringing a pregnancy to term could put her into heart failure and cause her to die. Neither woman could pay for an abortion, and so we, her doctors, had to petition the state Medicaid board, filling out paperwork—*including percentage estimates on each woman's prospects for survival*—and then wait for the ruling. In the end, Medicaid agreed to pay for the abortion in the first case, but not in the second. I was outraged at the helplessness I felt and at the powerlessness these very ill women had over the course of their lives. The standard used by the Medicaid panel was "risk of imminent death," and I remember dwelling on the absurdity of that: How close, exactly, does a poor woman need to be to death before the government allows her to get the medical support she needs?

These are the extreme cases. Most women who seek abortions are healthy and in the prime of their lives. Whatever factored into their decision making, they know what they want to do, or what they need to do by the time they enter my office, and they have gotten together the money required. These are the "lucky" ones. They don't need to submit to a process by which a doctor has to make estimates on survival rates and then wait for a ruling. Even so, they are, overwhelmingly, constrained. Abortion is the only personal decision that is subjected to this level of government oversight. More states require waiting periods before obtaining an abortion than buying a gun or getting married. Adults are presumed to be able to look after their own best interests and the best interests of the people who are depending on them. In every case except abortion, society bestows upon individuals this trust, *even if those individuals have demonstrated that they cannot be trusted to make good decisions.* The presumption undergirding abortion decision making is that women who have had sex and are accidentally or unintentionally pregnant can't be trusted to comprehend the consequential weight of their actions. The law requires them, like bad little girls, to "prove" to authorities that they have thought carefully about what they're about to do.

In health care, no other medical condition is treated this way. Take, for example, a patient diagnosed with a potentially terminal cancer and facing treatment options. Her life hangs in the balance, and no doctor can promise, with any certainty, what the outcome of any course may be. Before choosing a path, this patient has to consider—as all patients considering abortion must do—her own future. At this crossroads, what dreams does she still hope to fulfill? She also has to consider her present: Who depends on her? How much money does she have? What kind of support is available to her? Every physician understands that his or her job is to give that patient the most clear, accurate, up-to-date information about risks and outcomes, but that the choice—whether to pursue expensive, lifesaving treatment or not; whether to choose a diminishment in quality of life over a shorter life—is ultimately the patient's own to make, taking her age, her temperament, her finances, her life circumstances, and the wishes of her family into account. As with abortion, some patients find these decisions to be excruciating. And some choose a course of treatment without second thoughts. Some choose one path and then wish, mid-stream, that they had chosen another. No one—not doctors, not legislators, not picketers, or lobbyists—thinks to judge or shame or punish cancer patients for their decisions—even if those choices lead to death. Quite the opposite. Cancer treatment is spoken of in terms of heroics. A woman who decides not to pursue treatment and to shorten her life in order to be clear-minded for as long as possible is considered "brave." A woman who decides to take radical action, to undergo surgeries and try every experimental drug in the pipeline is a "warrior." Even patients with lung cancer are not blamed and judged for smoking in the same way that women who seek abortions are blamed for having sex. Abortion is the only health-care decision that pits a woman against her own self-interest and presumes to know better than she does what she "ought" to do. Paradoxically, a woman is venerated if she refuses lifesaving cancer treatment while pregnant but vilified if she chooses her own life over a pregnancy.

It bears repeating: one in three American women have had

abortions in their lifetimes. I have probably done more than ten thousand abortions in the past dozen years. With numbers that high, it's inevitable that some proportion of patients will regret their decision—though in my experience, this seldom happens. More often, a woman remembers her abortion as a bittersweet event: an incidence of having to do what was necessary. Unlike the government patriarchs, I do not presume to be able to protect a woman from her own regret. Nor do I try to. Regret is the natural consequence of life, lived in maturity, full of mistakes. An adult is entitled to have regrets. What I can do is try, in the abortion clinics where I work, to create a safe haven where a woman's decision making is not unduly influenced by other people's ideas about what's right or wrong, or the regrets they think she ought to have. A woman's regrets, if she has them, should be her own.

The political conversation about abortion has obliterated truth and crushed any nuanced understanding of what it means to live a human life. Abortion talk in public is so black and white, so bolstered by scientific falsehoods and medical semi-truths, and so distorted by a fog of sentimentality about women and their role as mothers, that it has begun to muddle the thinking even of people in favor of abortion rights. We need to call out these lies and obfuscations for what they are. For if we don't, if we don't hold those myths up to the light and dissect them with the cool, rational eye of a scientist, then we will continue to be lulled into a sense of complacency over the fate of women's lives, and the people who are cynically perpetuating the lies—the antis, who want to make abortion inaccessible again—will win. The stakes are that high. The antis want nothing less than to control women's fertility, not just poor women but all women, in a last-ditch effort to subjugate them. If a woman is not in control of her fertility, she is not in control of her life. On my journey to become an abortion provider, I have also increasingly become an outspoken advocate for truth. These two roles exist side by side. As a scientist and a public-health professional, I know what the data say. As a clinician, my interactions with women every day give me a front-row seat into the messy realities of their real lives. As an activist, I shout out the truths I see, an antidote to the lies that have proliferated unchecked.

One of the cultural falsehoods that I most rail against is this: each and every abortion is a terrible tragedy and every woman who chooses to have an abortion is therefore a tragic figure. In this popular narrative, women are helpless victims—and not clear-eyed individuals making a sensible choice to benefit themselves and the people around them. I know, from seeing women every day, how far this is from being true. Most of the women I see are utterly matter-of-fact about what they're doing. They're on my table because they need to be. But the "tragic heroine" narrative supports what I call the "politics of respectability," a cultural set of unexamined assumptions that go like this: Women who make autonomous decisions about their sexual pleasure and their fertility are "bad," and an unplanned or unintended pregnancy represents a grave error in judgment. The highest calling of every woman is to become a mother, and if a woman does not choose to become a mother then something is wrong with her—she is deficient somehow, not all there. And if the choice to have an abortion automatically puts a woman's fundamental competency into question, then it stands to reason (in the eyes of the antis and those who support them) that she must be protected from herself. It may be difficult in a misogynist culture to regard women who freely choose sex and who freely choose to have abortions when needed as free agents taking their lives into their own hands. But the alternative is to see them as less than fully human and requiring of paternalistic intervention.

Another so-called fact put forth by the antis is that "life begins at conception"—the justification for the ridiculous claim that abortion is murder. As a Christian and a scientist, I can authoritatively attest that life does not begin at conception. This notion, that the union of the egg and sperm constitutes a new person at that moment, reflects a religious belief—and a deeply held one. But the fact is, as Justice Harry Blackmun so eloquently wrote way back in 1973, in the majority opinion in *Roe v. Wade*, there is no historical, philosophical, theological, or even scientific consensus on when life begins. So while the modern Roman Catholic hierarchy might regard each instance of fertilization as a sacred event, this belief is not—and has never been—universal among Christians. A thousand years ago, it was common for people to believe, as the Greeks did, that fetuses only possessed what they called "a vegetable soul" up until forty to eighty days of gestation—at which point God imbued them with a human soul. Even Thomas Aquinas, who established much of what is contemporary Catholic theology, believed that abortion was homicide only after the moment of "ensoulment," at forty to eighty days (forty days for a boy and eighty for a girl). Until the rise to national prominence of the Moral Majority before the presidential election of 1980, "life begins at conception" was not central to mainstream Protestant belief, and abortion was not explicitly forbidden.

The fact is that for most of modern Western history, abortion—which until the advent of modern surgical procedures in the twentieth century involved the ingestion of toxic herbs, roots, or potions to "restore menses"—has been regarded by common law as the legal and moral prerogative of pregnant women up until the moment of "quickening," the first maternal perception of fetal movement in utero, which occurs at around twenty weeks. Indeed, the first anti-abortion laws were enacted, in the middle of the nineteenth century, to protect women from buying and drinking poisons peddled to them by charlatans and not because jurists had any opinion about the so-called rights of any early-stage embryo or fetus. But this falsehood, that life begins at conception, has become so commonplace in our culture as to seem, even to certain supporters of abortion rights, as self-evident. And when a majority of voters unthinkingly concede its veracity, then legislators can enact all kinds of mischief, including proposing bills that equate "the rights" of a fetus at any stage post-fertilization with those of a living, breathing human person—and any termination of any pregnancy as murder. Laws in Missouri and Kansas say that "life begins at conception." Bills proposing that fetuses are people have come before legislatures in at least twenty-eight states. None have passed.

Based on what we know scientifically about human reproduction and embryology, I like to say that "life is a process." It is not a switch that turns on in an instant, like an electric light. Instead, life—before and after conception—is a galaxy of contingent, interconnected conditions that must be met in order for a single human to achieve progress, maturation, and fulfillment. Life happens, whether individual women and men choose to participate in the process of reproduction or not. The scientific truth, which touches every living thing in the natural world, is that, in the process of life, from fertilization until death, all sorts of events can arise that interrupt maturation. All beings perish for all kinds of reasons. But that finitude does not in every case equal murder. It is worth mentioning

here, though it may seem obvious, that the advocates of capital punishment in this country, who are frequently the same people who
oppose abortion rights, do not regard a death sentence—in which a
living, breathing human life is extinguished by the state—as "murder." Instead, they call it "justice." The hypocrisy of the political
right on capital punishment and abortion is more evidence, in my
opinion, that we cannot adjudicate these questions of "life" in the
realm of opinion and religious belief. Science is the only judge before which each and every party stands entirely equal.

· · ·

I approach my adversaries with compassion for their faith, but
armed with science. One sunny day in the spring of 2016, during
my lunch hour at the Tuscaloosa clinic, I went over to the University
of Alabama to help out the campus chapter of Unite for Reproductive & Gender Equity (URGE), the organization formerly known
as Choice USA, founded by the trailblazer Gloria Steinem. (I sit on
the board.) URGE was staging a rally at the campus student center around LGBTQ and reproductive rights. As I descended into
the paved quad from the parking garage, I saw my friends—young
women wearing shorts, their tattoos showing on their shoulder
blades—standing around a collection of folding tables covered with
neat baskets and piles of badges, stickers, and handouts. Poster
board signs were taped to the edge of each table and hung, fluttering, down to the ground. I GOT 99 PROBLEMS, BUT PREGNANCY AIN'T
ONE, said one. Another showed a photo of a twisted coat hanger: WE
WON'T GO BACK! It was near the end of the school year, exam time,
on a southern campus known more for football than progressive
activism, and my young feminist friends were having a hard time

holding the attention of their peers. So I stepped up, still wearing my green scrubs, and extemporaneously offered a few words to the people busily crisscrossing the quad: "We don't talk about sex in Alabama, and we sure as hell don't talk about abortion. But abortion care is something we need to get over in terms of stigma and shame. When you need it, you need it." And then I paraphrased Dr. King, who always gives me words when I am at a loss. I urged students to stand up with their classmates for reproductive justice. "It's not where you stand in moments of ease. It's where you stand in moments of controversy."

A small crowd had gathered, including a tight-knit group of young men and women who represented the anti-abortion group on campus. They looked no different from any other group of college students in cutoffs and sneakers and with unruly hair, and they listened to me respectfully. But afterward, when I had finished my short speech, they approached me and we inevitably got into a heated talk about when life begins. One of the women had found my remarks to the crowd—especially "When you need it, you need it"—to be callous and offensive. I respectfully but assertively engaged with her, and she became tearfully frustrated and ran away, still shouting at me. I can understand why the antis like to insist that "life begins at conception." It's a simple way to comprehend human reproduction, and because of its simplicity, it offers moral clarity. What I tried to impress upon those students that day is that the scientific truth about life is complicated—but complication doesn't conflict with a deeply moral, or even religious, orientation. It's just that a nuanced moral stance requires wrestling with science and God in a way that might be difficult. It might take some time.

An egg, unfertilized, is alive. And sperm are alive. The human beings who generated those cells, which are called gametes, are also alive. These humans move and think; their cells consume and create energy. Men and women who have engaged in sexual intercourse are healthy, or not; they have good nutrition, or not. They carry with them the DNA of generations of ancestors who were also once alive. Within that DNA are maps or codes for possible future outcomes: brilliance, depression, obesity, schizophrenia, heart disease—all these living secrets are contained in each human cell, whether fertilized or not. So the idea that life begins at conception is already false: life begins long before conception with the lives that enabled those gametes to come into being. But let me continue.

The sperm and the egg meet, most often, in the fallopian tube, after which the fertilized egg takes a three- or four-day journey down the tube and into the uterus, where, in order to become a healthy pregnancy, it must implant itself into the uterine lining. Some large number—no one knows how large—of fertilized eggs never make it to this next step. They are fertilized, but they fail to safely travel. Or, in an ectopic pregnancy, they are fertilized and implant themselves right there in the tube, where they will not survive, and where their rupture can cause serious injury to the woman—bleeding, even death. Or they travel but fail to implant. In that last case, the uterine lining sheds, a woman has her period, and she never knows that, in the dark cavern of her body, a "conception" has occurred. There is, in other words, a huge amount of natural waste that goes into the achievement of a "normal" pregnancy. Do all these conceptions qualify as "life" as the antis define it? A "person" with rights equal to a woman's rights?

Similarly: as many as one in five implanted embryos fail to thrive, resulting in miscarriage sometime between six and twelve weeks of conception. Women who want to be pregnant know this well; that's why so many decide not to tell their friends and family about an intended pregnancy until that pregnancy is further along. These women know that intention does not equal certainty. Is an embryo that fails to thrive "life"? On the same level as a healthy newborn? Or on the same level as the woman carrying it?

A full-term pregnancy lasts forty weeks, on average. And up until at least twenty-two weeks, the fetus is not "viable." That is, it cannot—it will not—survive outside the uterus, not with the assistance of medical technology, as in a respirator, and not with the spiritual support of earnest and hopeful prayer. Not ever. Up until twenty-two weeks, fetal development is insufficient to sustain life. A baby born at that gestational age cannot breathe. Its body weight cannot support life. Its skin is permeable. The antis may want to call a twenty-two-week fetus a "person," but if born, it will die.

The antis don't want to hear this, but "life" is a gray area. There is a period, between about twenty-two and twenty-five weeks of gestational age, during which "life" is a vague state. A fetus may or may not be viable in that period, and there's no way to reliably predict outcomes. A fetus born during this period is not definitively consigned life. Nor is it destined to die. Depending on various different factors—its weight, its lung development, the health of its mother, the expertise of the doctors in charge, and the technological capacity of the neonatal facility—it may live. Or not. And if it lives, it may grow up into a healthy adult, or it may suffer, afflicted with extensive organ and brain damage, and die young. These are the medical facts, having nothing to do with religious belief, or the power of prayer, or the hopes of parents to raise beautiful children. The American Congress of Obstetricians and Gynecologists does not recommend trying to resuscitate babies born at twenty-three weeks. At twenty-four weeks, doctors understand that it's a crapshoot and they let the parents, together with their attending doctors, decide. At twenty-five weeks, the American Medical Association recommends resuscitation. But within these guidelines, doctors understand that "life" is not assured and that its "sanctity" is merely a hope.

Also in the second trimester, a small percentage of fetuses are discovered to have anomalies so severe that they will not survive outside the uterus. Very often these anomalies are not discovered until after twenty weeks because, up until that point, major organ systems are too small and indistinct for sonogram technology to capture them. Sometimes a fetus has anencephaly: it has a brain stem but is missing some or most of the brain or cranium. Or it will have renal agenesis: no kidneys. Or something we doctors call "limb-body wall complex," in which organs develop outside the fetal body cavity. Or neural tube defects, such as encephalocele, in which parts of the brain protrude through the skull. Or lethal skeletal dysplasia, in which spinal growth is severely impaired. These are the real tragedies. In most of these cases, the would-be parents are hoping for a healthy child and are informed, when the pregnancy is more than halfway along, that the fetus is impaired. This information causes excruciating psychic pain and trauma for would-be parents, who most often have planned for and greatly desire this birth. To paint a clear picture: in the fourteen states that have passed twenty-week-abortion bans since 2010, a woman carrying a fetus with a strong heartbeat—but afflicted with a condition that consigns it, inevitably, to death immediately upon birth—*cannot* choose to legally terminate her pregnancy.

When I was a resident training in ob-gyn, I witnessed the full-term birth of a baby with what's known as Potter syndrome—a dramatic decrease of amniotic fluid in utero usually related to the failure of the kidneys to develop properly. The woman in question was young, about eighteen years old, and her mother worked in housekeeping at the hospital. The anomaly had not been discovered until a gestational age of nineteen weeks. Abortion would normally have been the recommended course, but this woman was a fundamentalist Christian, and she opted to bring the pregnancy to term because, as she told me, she was praying for a miracle. As a healthy pregnancy progresses, the placenta and the amniotic fluid work together as the fetus's circulatory and elimination systems; they are the fetus's heart, lungs, and stomach until birth, when the baby's own organs take over. But in Potter syndrome, the absence of kidneys results in virtually no amniotic fluid production, which in turn results in the absence of fetal lung development. This baby was born at thirty-nine weeks—a girl, as I recall—and I stood by and watched, in horror, as she died. She grunted and made efforts to inhale as the oxygen hunger built up in her body, but there was no lung capacity. Born at term, the baby could feel pain, and, even if she couldn't interpret anything like self-consciousness, she must have felt all the anxiety and panic that would accompany suffocating to death. In this case, an absolute reverence for life led to a situation that, to my eyes, consisted of nothing less than pure cruelty.

In my conversation with the young anti-abortion activists at the University of Alabama that day, I presented fatal fetal anomalies as clear-cut cases for the necessity of preserving abortion rights up to and beyond twenty weeks. They countered that sometimes miracles happen that allow these fetuses to survive. Yes, I answered, maybe. But most of the time they don't. And the students were forced to concede that, sometimes maybe, abortion does not equal murder. And then I brought my argument home: If you can agree that certain medical conditions might justify abortion, then how can you exclude social, or personal, or financial conditions? If abortion is permissible in the case of a fatal fetal anomaly, then why not in the case of a homicidal, battering partner? Or a dire lack of resources? Or a drug dependency? How can the state adjudicate the circumstances of a woman's life at all?

When I'm doing counseling in the Mississippi clinic, what I like to say to women is this: You are pregnant. You have a decision to make, and the way I see it, you have some very clear choices. You can carry this pregnancy to term and become a parent. You can carry this pregnancy to term and put the baby up for adoption. You can decide not to carry this pregnancy to term. Each one of these paths is paved with uncertainty and unforeseen outcomes. You may decide to become a parent and then miscarry, or give birth to a child who contracts a fatal disease or winds up in jail. Alternatively, you might decide to become a parent and raise a child who becomes the president of the United States or a prominent abortion doctor. You may choose to have an abortion and regret the choice for the rest of your life. Or you may win an Olympic gold medal in the 400 or become teacher of the year or meet someone next week with whom you want to raise a family and spend the rest of your life. In the large and interconnected set of biological preconditions—conditions and processes that, taken collectively, are "life"— there is no right course. In the process of "life" there are many risks and no guarantees, so the only thing I ask is that you press mute on the noise and the judgment from the voices out there—from the picketers on the street and the folks at your own kitchen table, and even my voice other than the information I'm providing—to decide, based on your own life, and your desires, and your resources what is right for you.

. . .

Another truth: A fetus is not "a person." It is not, therefore, entitled to the rights of "a person." This ought to be obvious, and yet since 2008, when an advocacy group called Personhood USA was established, an avalanche of bills perennially come before state legislatures, proposing to write "fetal personhood" into law—an unconscionable, immoral waste of time and taxpayer dollars. In 2016, "personhood" bills were introduced in Alabama, Colorado, Mississippi, Rhode Island, Iowa, Maryland, Missouri, South Carolina, and Virginia. The only state in which such a bill has passed has been Kansas, which in 2013 affirmed the Pro-Life Protection Act, declaring that "life begins at conception." No such bill has ever succeeded on the federal level.

This personhood mischief, which has created so much senseless noise in the abortion conversation, has been enabled, ironically, by technological progress. Humans have developed in utero the same way for two hundred thousand years, ever since *Homo sapiens* showed up on the planet. And for all of those millennia, the moral content of that biological reality has remained the same. For most of human history, pregnancy was a black box, a process that evolved, invisibly and mysteriously, within the body of a woman, apparent to outsiders only in that over time it caused her belly to magnificently protrude.

But sonogram technology, first developed in the late 1950s and in wide use by the early 2000s, allowed doctors—and ultimately their patients—to look inside the black box, and, as a consequence, to impose personlike attributes on even the youngest fetuses. The heart-stopping 1965 spread of in utero photos by *Life* magazine showed the anthropomorphizing process of human development and enhanced the moral cloudiness of the abortion issue. Now in their propaganda, the antis might use these photos and embellish them with the language of Jeremiah: *Before I formed you in the womb, I knew you.* By the early 1980s, sonogram pictures were a routine part of prenatal care, of extreme utility to ob-gyns, who might use them in early diagnosis of Down syndrome and ensure healthy fetal development, and a delight to so many expectant parents who would go home from the doctor's office and post the early sonogram pictures on their refrigerators with colorful magnets. "Look!" a prospective parent might say, gazing upon the magnified to larger-than-scale fetus on a black-and-white computer screen. "It's sleeping on its back! It has its ankles crossed! It looks like Grandma Nellie!" This is an understandable expression of desire, but it conflates sentimental yearning about parenthood and children with biological truth. To people who desperately want a baby, these images may seem to confirm their deepest hope: here is their child; a relative; a link to the past and to the future; a person who might be blue-eyed like her mother or athletic like her father. That the fetus has human features—fingers, eyelids, toes, ankles—only enhances the illusion that this is already a baby, their baby. But to refer to the fetus in utero as a baby is inaccurate. It reflects a hope, not a reality. In reference to a fetus, "baby" is a cultural term, not a scientific one.

Truth, however, doesn't matter to the antis. Early on, they saw in the very detailed sonogram photographs an opportunity to manipulate the public. They capitalized on people's predisposition to imagine fetuses as babies and exploited it, illustrating all their propaganda with high-resolution sonogram images of fetuses in utero:

sleeping, sucking their thumbs, seeming to smile or express aston-
ishment or surprise. In 1984, antis began screening a twenty-eight-
minute film called *The Silent Scream* at their gatherings. In the
grainy black-and-white video, a twelve-week fetus is purportedly
aborted by vacuum aspiration while a narrator describes the fetus
thrashing, recoiling, and even screaming in fear and pain. (Fact-
check: The brain of a twelve-week fetus is not developed enough to
feel pain or fear or to deliberately control the movement of limbs.)
By 1996, anti-abortion forces were passing laws requiring women
to look at their sonograms before having an abortion, in the hope
of encouraging maternal bonding. A woman could not possibly
choose abortion, the antis argued, once she saw in the sonogram
image "a separate human being with brain waves, moving arms,
kicking legs, and a beating heart," in the words of one anti-abortion
website. Now, when David, the protester who every day devotes
himself to standing outside the Montgomery clinic shouts, "Don't
kill your baby!" to women entering through the front doors, he is
holding a high-resolution poster of a thirty-plus-week fetus with a
double intention—to represent that image as a fetus at nine weeks of
gestation, which is utterly false, and to intimate that abortions are
routinely and indiscriminately done at a stage when the pregnancy
could survive. In what I see as an entirely unethical and immoral
conflation, the antis have manufactured plastic models of six-week
fetuses to use as visual aids in their protests. These don't look like
fetuses at all: they look like teeny-tiny little pink and brown dolls.
In reality, a six-week-old fetal pole and gestational sac are as big as
a lima bean. It has the earliest notable cardiac activity, but an un-
developed heart and a very rudimentary circulatory system. But the
antis are falsely leading people to believe that a fetus, at six weeks,

looks like a baby—with all the component parts that a human being has. This is more than manipulation. It's a blatant lie.

Having walked past the antis' posters every day of my work life for more than a dozen years, I have begun to develop a new insight about what these images might unconsciously mean. I have begun to see these manipulations as a twenty-first-century version of ancient patriarchal misconceptions about how babies are made, pseudoscientific fables that served to protect men's exclusive rights to fetal ownership. In the earliest efforts to understand reproduction, people believed that women were merely earth—potting soil—contributing nothing at all to the development of a new living being. With their "seed," as it was known, men contributed everything, from physical appearance to intelligence. Residing in the head of every sperm was a fully formed human being in miniature, a homunculus, which would be "planted" inside the woman. She was the man's property: she existed to bear children for him, and any interruption or violation of that role was regarded as stealing, a violation of property rights—the same as trespassing on a farmer's field and stealing his corn or his wheat. I believe these posters unconsciously rearticulate that ancient claim: fetuses are miniature people, belonging exclusively to the men in charge. The men, therefore, are within their rights to punish anyone—including pregnant women and abortion doctors, like me—whom they regard as thieves or poachers.

Truth: Until twenty-nine weeks, a fetus can't feel anything like pain. This is the established opinion of a 2005 clinical review in the *Journal of the American Medical Association*, and the American College of Obstetricians and Gynecologists agrees. Both consider the inability of a fetus to feel pain before the third trimester an established fact. And yet, despite the empirical evidence given by science, and not contradicted, the antis continue to disseminate their own version of "truth"—which is to say, lies—and to pass laws that support an entirely false idea about what fetuses in utero can "feel." Of the twenty-two states that ban abortion after a certain number of weeks, fifteen of them do so on the grounds that a fetus may feel pain. Of the thirty-five states that require mandated pre-abortion counseling, twelve require the woman to be given information about the fetus's capacity for pain, and, in some cases, offer fetal anesthesia—despite the fact that there is no established medical protocol for fetal anesthesia during an abortion. It is not a thing that doctors do. In 2013, a federal appeals court struck down Arizona's fetal pain law, but the Supreme Court declined to hear the state's appeal—which means that every state without a fetal pain law can now enact one, albeit vulnerable to a federal court challenge.

This recasting of fetuses as babies—tiny people who feel pain and are in need of society's protection—amounts to nothing more than a cynical marketing campaign, conveniently dovetailing with a shift in the way the antis are waging their war on abortion rights. In the first two decades after *Roe*, anti-abortion forces could be easily caricatured as haters: middle-aged, red-faced white people hollering Bible verses at vulnerable women and turning out in droves to elect Republican candidates committed to overthrowing *Roe*.

At around the time that George W. Bush was running for re-election, the public face of evangelical Christianity began to change. A new generation of young Christians, alienated from their fathers' punitive and judgmental language on abortion and homosexuality, hoped to recast their activism, rhetorically and strategically, in gentler terms. On abortion, they weren't changing their minds. In fact, this new generation of Christians was even more conservative, less conciliatory, than their parents had been. But they discovered that they might make more headway in their fight against abortion rights if they stopped behaving like bullies and started, instead, to frame their arguments in terms of Christian love. Just as a new generation of Christians seemed to express openness toward their homosexual brothers and sisters with the phrase "hate the sin, love the sinner," anti-abortion activists changed their tactics, too. Their love for sinners encompassed "fallen" women. But that love did not supersede their Christian concern for vulnerable fetuses—who, the rhetoric went, had no one to protect them. The anti-abortion movement very cynically began to co-opt the language of the human rights movement.

"Our legislation focuses on the humanity of the unborn child," said Carol Tobias, the president of National Right to Life after the Supreme Court overturned the abortion clinic restrictions in Texas as unconstitutional. In anti-abortion messaging, a dramatic conflation has occurred, obscuring all truth. Now all fetuses, everywhere, are the same as "babies"—and abortion is murder not just in individual cases but on a worldwide scale. Now a woman who chooses abortion is not just culpable and irresponsible. She (and the doctor who performed her abortion) are participants in a systematic evil, cogs in a machinery of genocide that deprive innocent fetuses of "life."

CHAPTER 9

Black Genocide and the
White Majority

Nothing enrages me more than the antis' most recent strategic gambit: the black genocide movement. Launched in its current iteration in 2009 by white anti-abortion activists in Georgia, it is a craven and cynical effort to get black people to regard the clinical practice of abortion—as well as the whole abortion rights movement—as an assault by white America on blacks. Banking on the fact that 37 percent of the women who seek abortion in America are black, the black genocide movement positions Planned Parenthood as the main perpetrator of this genocide and the birth control pioneer Margaret Sanger as its primary architect. The black genocide movement is nothing more than a conspiracy theory pretending that abortion is a white plot to kill black babies and that by raising this "awareness" in black communities, it is protecting millions of black lives from slaughter. As an African American abortion provider who grew up in poverty, I take this accusation—that I am complicit in this white "plot"—very personally. It is true that because poor women and women of color have less access to reliable birth control and health care, they are more likely than more privileged women to have unplanned pregnancies. They are also less likely to have taken comprehensive sex ed in school, and the conditions of their lives are chaotic and unstable, which can lead to complex, less than socially acceptable decision making. They probably choose medication abortion less than privileged women (although good data here is hard to find), because they tend to make their abortion decisions at a later gestational age. These women walk into abortion clinics more often than privileged women—not necessarily because they don't want a child or another child (many of them do), but because the circumstances of their lives are constraining and prohibitive. Women of all races and socioeconomic groups cite multiple reasons for seeking an abortion: lack of financial resources, relationship instability, more children at home. But this multiplicity of factors disproportionately afflict poor women and women of color. I see it all the time.

The implication that, in their effort to preserve their own sanity and resources and to save their own lives, these women are murderers, makes me want to lash out, like Jesus overthrowing the tables in the Temple. The black genocide movement is a trumped-up play to gain political advantage. Cynically disguised as civil rights, it targets the most vulnerable women and pits their pregnancy against their own self-interest. In doing so, the black genocide movement only serves to compound the misery of people who are already living in circumstances of pain and deprivation.

I first saw the black genocide billboards on highways running through mainly African American neighborhoods in Atlanta and New York. One of them had a gigantic photograph of a beautiful

African American child. It said, BLACK CHILDREN ARE AN ENDANGERED SPECIES. Another said, THE MOST DANGEROUS PLACE FOR A BLACK BABY IS IN THE WOMB. A third had a picture of President Barack Obama and read, EVERY 21 MINUTES, OUR NEXT POSSIBLE LEADER IS ABORTED. These signs prey on black women's traditional sense of responsibility to their community and imply that they have some kind of higher duty—higher than to themselves—to continue a pregnancy.

In 2009, a white pro-life filmmaker named Mark Crutcher produced a documentary-style propaganda piece called *Maafa 21*, which equates abortion by black women to slavery and the eugenics experiments of the first half of the twentieth century. Positioned as a "civil rights" film, it circulated widely among various African American groups. After it came out, I read an interview with a young, well-educated student at Morris Brown College who said that, having seen the movie, she now understood there was a conspiracy to kill black people, implying that she'd factor that line of reasoning into her decision-making process should she ever find herself contemplating an abortion. This young woman was on track to realize her hopes and dreams, and it anguished me that based on these lies she was willing to go off track, to risk poverty for herself and for a prospective child, which was precisely what the white purveyors of these lies hoped she would do.

Now when I see a patient like this in one of the clinics where I work, and I sense that she's wavering based not on her own inner voice but because of some propaganda she encountered somewhere, I try to rebuild her self-esteem and her dignity. I tell her that her decision to care for herself is not in conflict with any duty she may or may not have to other people who look like her, and that the shame she feels is a product of outside forces who want her to feel this way—

not because people care about her but because as a poor woman or a woman of color, she's an easy target. She can be made into an example to further someone else's agenda. I remind her that before she can ever help anyone else, she must first help herself. I seldom see women who genuinely want to change their minds based on this propaganda. Most are resolute—they are committed to their course of action—but are distressed by the social pressures they feel from such forces as the black genocide movement. I encourage these women to act on their own behalf and to feel the power of their own agency.

The truth, I am convinced, is that the people behind the black genocide movement, like Priests for Life and Life Dynamics, do not care about black babies and black women. These are often the same people who want to do away with public housing, who won't support state-sponsored child care. Theirs is a feigned concern. They are using women of color as pawns in a much bigger game. For they understand what too few of the foot soldiers in the abortion debate do. In abortion politics, all women are sisters, linked by their ability to bear children. If the antis can change the terms of the abortion debate, framing it as a systemic racism perpetrated by big health-care institutions against black people, then they can change the laws around abortion and no one will intervene, not even the white women who need abortions, too.

Their goal—I'm preaching now, I can't help it—is not, actually, to curtail abortion services for poor women and women of color. It's to limit access to abortion for *all* women, including, and especially, white women. Because the thing all too many white anti-abortion activists really want, which they can't say out loud, is for white women to have more babies, in order to push back against the browning of America. As we march toward the reality that, by

2050, no one racial or ethnic group will hold a proportional majority in this country, racial suicide paranoia abounds. And for the white racist legislators in the red states, nothing is more threatening than a majority-brown country; it strips them of their historic power. The prospect of being outnumbered is what enabled the Tea Party's mutiny of Congress in 2010 after the election of Barack Obama, America's first black president, allowing it to cripple the Republican establishment; render the first major-party female presidential candidate powerless; and enable the rise of the racist, nationalistic, and misogynistic Donald Trump. The white people who are still in charge believe that if their women don't start having lots of babies, they—the white patriarchs—are going to become obsolete.

A hundred years ago, a white politician with this same fear who hoped to exert control over female fertility would just say so. In his 1905 speech "On American Motherhood," Theodore Roosevelt encouraged white women to do their duty and have at least two children, or else contemplate "race suicide." In these times, such a bald articulation of racist values is impossible. Too many of their own women are working and going to school, running businesses, running for political office, and taking birth control pills: any outward pressure on daughters or sisters or wives to have more children would be risible. And so the white men in charge have invented a work-around. They've tied their antipathy toward abortion together with civil rights and the Black Lives Matter movement. They understand that by curtailing abortion for black women they curtail it for white women, too. It's a sleight of hand, a misdirection. The way I see it, the attack on abortion rights is nothing less than an effort to put all women back in their place.

CHAPTER 10

My Sisters' Keeper

In 2011, an acquaintance named Susan Yanow approached me with an idea. Susan lives in Boston and is a fierce abortion rights activist, a one-person wrecking crew for patriarchy. She conceived a project that, in the manner of medical-residency program admissions, matches abortion doctors with the clinics nationwide most desperate for skilled help. If an abortion clinic in an embattled state is struggling to stay open because local physicians, fearing physical harm and the negative fallout of stigma and shame on their families, refuse to work there, then Yanow will send them a willing and capable doctor from out of state. The result is a small band of warriors, perhaps as many as a hundred, who regularly fly in to the most dangerous states—in the South, the Midwest, and the Great Plains, where their lives and reputations are in peril—perform abortions, and then fly out. Most of these doctors are women, and they split their time between the clinics and their practices in ob-gyn or family medicine. But a few, like me, are full-time "circuit providers." They are always on the road. They log sometimes as many as one thousand miles a week. These are the indefatigable special forces of the abortion rights movement, living out of anonymous hotels, sometimes wearing masks to protect their identities and bulletproof vests to preserve their lives. Operation Save America, the twenty-first-century iteration of Operation Rescue, which organized the Summer of Mercy in Wichita and whose founder, Randall Terry, implied after the assassination of Dr. Tiller that he deserved what he got, tracks these practitioners and exposes them when it can. One famous circuit provider, whom I won't name for obvious reasons, always traveled wearing a Three Stooges mask. Operation Rescue found her out and posted her photo, her name, as well as that of her elderly mother, on its website. Susan wondered if I might want to join this small army of traveling doctors to serve the women for whom getting a safe and legal abortion was nearly impossible. I was intrigued.

At the time, I was living in Washington, D.C. In 2009, I had left my job as the director of Family Planning at Washington Hospital Center to become the medical director of five busy Planned Parenthood clinics in metro D.C. But I was in transition again, putting together a schedule as an independent contractor, working in abortion clinics in Washington and Philadelphia. I had been at Planned Parenthood for two and a half years, doing abortions for women on a daily basis and providing the medical leadership for the clinics. But my appetite for advocacy was growing. I had a long-standing interest in public health. In clinical work you can improve lives on an individual level; a public-health approach aims for system-wide change, and in the years immediately following my training at Harvard, I spent three years working for the California Department of Health Services, studying the data on domestic violence, maternal mortality, black infant health, and teen pregnancy. The professional question that tantalized me was this: How do we improve health prospects for women by attacking behaviors, perceptions, and, yes, laws?

Planned Parenthood had given me opportunities to speak out. I traveled with the organization's president, Cecile Richards, when she made calls on the Hill, and when President Obama was trying to pass his health-care law, Planned Parenthood tapped me to protest the Stupak-Pitts Amendment, which restricted the provision of abortion care for women receiving government insurance. (Despite our advocacy, the amendment passed.) I was grateful for these opportunities to advocate, but I found that my connection with Planned Parenthood constrained me as well, for there were times when my mission and my employer's were not precisely aligned. In 2010, for example, the far-right television personality Glenn Beck began traveling the country in what he called a "civil rights" campaign—"We are on the side of individual freedoms and liberties," he said, "and, dammit, we will reclaim the civil rights movement!"—appropriating the legacy and the rhetoric of Dr. King to further an anti-feminist, anti-gay, anti-abortion agenda. He was even traveling in cahoots with Alveda King, a niece of Dr. King, who worked for Priests for Life as an agent of the black genocide movement. Beck's campaign was odious to me, especially the irreverent appropriation of civil rights language and iconography. When he made his station stop in the District of Columbia, I wanted to meet him with a full-throated rebuttal. But at Planned Parenthood headquarters, strategists had decided that their optimal play was to keep temperatures low and to meet Beck with silence. Sensing their reticence to engage on this issue but personally convinced this pernicious and disrespectful ploy had to be addressed in an urban center with a large African American population, I expressed my intent to speak out as a black man and physician on behalf of my community. As a compromise, I proposed that I speak my mind outside my Planned Parenthood affiliation. They accepted.

Not every unit in an army can fight every battle, and I decried Beck's hypocrisies under my own banner. Don't misunderstand. I am a loyal Planned Parenthood partisan and will fight with and for them at every opportunity. But the incident helped me see that if advocacy was to become a greater part of my mission, I had better be unfettered by organizational obligations—and so I continue to join with Planned Parenthood as an ally. By detaching myself from my full-time job, I could continue to do what I loved—engage with patients on a personal level and provide them with expert care—while also standing up for what I believed. I could also work more seamlessly with a number of strong organizations doing necessary justice work on reproductive, race, and gender-equality issues. And so I went out on my own, took charge of my own health insurance, retirement plan, and also my time. I worked in clinics four, five, and sometimes six days a week, but always preserved one day for activism, to meet with other activist organizations, to strategize, to write, or to speak in public. I increased my contact with the advocacy group Physicians for Reproductive Health, and regularly led young doctors on visits to the Hill, where, dressed in our white coats, we would meet with congressional staff, drop off fact sheets, and tell our patients' stories. I sometimes felt hokey walking around the nation's capital in a lab coat, but I was comfortable, too. From my days as a proselytizing Christian, I had long ago developed the thick skin needed for knocking on doors. When I looked around the well-waxed hallways, I saw Americans of every color, dressed in the uniforms of their profession—military or law enforcement officers, the winner of the Miss Agribusiness competition wearing her sash— pressing upon their representatives the importance of their cause.

Susan's mission dovetailed nicely with my expanding vision of my life as a symbiotic combination of clinical work and advocacy, and I filled out forms she sent me that would match me with a clinic with the greatest need. But when her system connected me with Jackson Women's Health clinic in Mississippi—the only abortion clinic in the entire state, which at the time retained just one doctor who flew in a couple days a week from his home in Charlotte, North Carolina, and who wore a Halloween mask as he drove from the airport to downtown Jackson, my first reaction was "No." And my second reaction was more emphatic: *"Hell, no."*

At the time, my mind was set. I was nearly fifty, after all. Since Hawaii, I had spent most of my professional life in the North, in liberal, urban communities. I had come to enjoy all the advantages these environments provided me. For one thing, it was not anomalous in Washington or Philadelphia to be an African American abortion provider, although as a male member of that professional group, I would always be somewhat of a unicorn. In Washington, it was easy enough to move around inconspicuously, to make friends, and to live among people who shared my commitment to broad-mindedness. And my chosen occupation did not exclude me from any social circle (or any friendship or any romantic attachment, for that matter). In the hubbub of Washington, D.C., what I missed of the South as a loss of a common language, an agreed-upon sense of gentility and manners, was more than compensated for by an openness about almost everything. In Washington, I could be looser and more frank about who I was and what I did every day. I could say the word "abortion" without raising eyebrows. I could talk about what I believed. The Northeast left me satisfied. As I liked to say back then, Alabama was a better place to be from than to be in.

Also, Mississippi had a serious public-relations problem, in my mind. I knew too well, having been raised in the South, how historic disagreements around politics and principle there can fester and then erupt, suddenly, into violence—sometimes lethal violence. And Mississippi had long been the symbolic epicenter of racial violence. I had seen *Mississippi Burning* at least five times, but even before I saw the movie I knew, of course, about the terrible deaths of James Chaney, Michael Schwerner, and Andrew Goodman, the middle of the night traffic stop by the Ku Klux Klan—the gunshots, the terrible lynching. While attending medical school in Iowa, I frequently traveled by car from Birmingham to Iowa City, driving a route that took me through the northeast corner of Mississippi, through rural counties with names like Prentiss, Lee, and Alcorn, and as I logged the miles, the images of those assassinated young men haunted me. The countryside abutting those stretches of highway seemed to be populated by the overworked, starving ghosts of my people, and I always told friends that I didn't like to drive through Mississippi: the trees were too tall and the nights too dark. As a black man, I had a primal, visceral fear of the entire state. Emigrating there as an African American abortion provider was inconceivable to me.

Then I thought better of my instinctive negativity. "If I'm going to say no to this, I better know what I'm turning down," I said to myself, and in August 2011, I flew to Jackson from Washington, D.C., to check out Mississippi's last open abortion clinic. I boarded the plane with some anxiety, fearful that I was going back in time, to a place where white men wore skinny ties and their hair slicked back, and people like me were called "colored" or "Negro." I was afraid, to be frank, that by looking at me, people could see through my skin and discern who I was and what I did all day. Instead, what I found was a plane disproportionately full of black people, just regular folks, traveling home. And when I arrived in Jackson, I was bowled over—smitten—almost immediately. Waiting for me at the small airport, by the curb, was Shannon Brewer, the clinic's administrator. Young, African American, and whip smart, Shannon reminded me of Earnestine. Our connection was immediate. Shannon was warm but serious. She had worked her way up through every function of the clinic; she had never been to college but had washed glassware and instruments, counseled patients and held their hands in the procedure room. Now she was running the place: in charge of patient appointments and paperwork, the doctors' schedules, and the budget. Chatting all the while, Shannon drove me to the clinic, a stand-alone sandstone building on a hipster block of Jackson, which the owner, Diane Derzis, had, in a blatant gesture of defiance against conformity and social conservatism, painted Pepto-Bismol pink. There, Shannon introduced me to Miss Betty, an older woman who did the counseling. Miss Betty's manner was open and endearing; she was like the cool aunt you wish you had. She had grown up in Mississippi during the civil rights era, and in the 1980s had helped launch Jesse Jackson's presidential campaign. As she matured, Miss Betty had shifted the focus of her activism from civil rights to reproductive rights, and she approached this work with the calm, assertive confidence of a person with a calling. What struck me was that everyone I met in connection with the clinic was a woman. And almost everyone was black.

The city of Jackson was also not what I expected at all. It was in the midst of a progressive renaissance. The clinic was within walking distance of a health food store and a pub that served artisanal beer. I never ate there but, right down the street, was a revamped old service station that was now a very popular and creatively named barbecue joint called Pigs & Pint. Once a flash point for racial conflict in the country, the city now has a black mayor. And the manners and customs of the people I met down there—well, they reminded me of family, of people I already knew. Shannon and Miss Betty told me about the women who came to Jackson Women's Health seeking care—women living in the Delta, in abject poverty, sometimes driving for four or five hours on country roads to get there. Mississippi has some of the highest rates of teen pregnancy in the country, as well as some of the highest infant and maternal mortality rates. Nationally, the poverty rate is about 14 percent, but in Mississippi, it's 23. And among black people in Mississippi, it's 36. These stories, these data points, reinforced my sense of belonging to this world. This was a place, and people, I already knew, down deep in my bones. And then Shannon and Miss Betty told me about their political activism. At that time, the Mississippi state legislature was considering a proposed "fetal personhood" ballot measure, like the bill pending in Colorado at that time. But the employees of this clinic, together with a coalition of other reproductive health activists, infertility specialists, advocates for victims of rape, and community organizers among women of color had organized a countermovement called Wake Up, Mississippi, a campaign to articulate the vast and devastating impact on women that the passage of such a bill would have. And the bill failed. These were health-care workers who were also civil rights activists, and they buttressed my present sense of calling. I saw that without this clinic, kept open by these people, the women of Mississippi would have no options. When Diane Derzis drove up from her summer home in Mobile to meet me, I was bowled over. Charismatic, defiant, and super-smart, Diane had been trained as a lawyer and worked for years as a lobbyist in the area of reproductive rights. She owned clinics in Jackson, Birmingham, and Virginia—committed to the rights of women and to fighting like hell for their right to abortion care.

I flew back to Washington, feeling totally engaged and energized—understanding my vocation in a whole new way. In Washington, in Philadelphia, there were more than enough abortion providers. The emotional dynamics and inner conflicts around abortion in these urban hubs might be the same for the women who needed them, and the medical procedure was, of course, identical. But as in Hawaii, open clinics and qualified doctors were everywhere, and patients who had made the inner journey of deciding to have an abortion and then moved heaven and earth to be able to schedule an appointment were not at risk of having that procedure canceled or rescheduled arbitrarily because the one provider willing to work in their state had car trouble or was home sick with the flu. In Washington, D.C., if an abortion provider doesn't show up for work, a woman can still get her abortion—most likely on the same day. In Mississippi, if the single doctor on the schedule in the only clinic in the state has a family emergency or a sore throat, then every woman sitting in the waiting room that day is out of luck; forced to reorganize her life again to come back another time. I saw how much I could contribute in Mississippi. I called Susan and told her yes, I would travel back and forth. I understood that by committing to a schedule of regular trips outside my safe zones, I was taking on more risk. I understood that as a black abortion provider in the South, I was making myself easy to see, easy to notice, easy to target—that I was essentially leaping from the frying pan and into the fire.

. . .

Working as an abortion provider in the South allowed me to see with my own eyes what I had long suspected. It wasn't just the provincial white legislators who were to blame for the raft of new laws restricting access to abortion, especially for women who live in Bible Belt states. It was whole flanks of the left (among them passionate abortion rights supporters) who found it easy to look away from the plight of their sisters or who were able to rationalize the new laws as, in some way, "reasonable." Partially, this was the result of a misbegotten political strategy.

In 2005, hoping to find common ground with those same social conservatives who elected George W. Bush, Democrats recalibrated their position on abortion. Instead of waging a righteous war on behalf of women and their constitutional rights to liberty and privacy, Democrats began to concede that abortion was a "difficult," even "tragic" choice. In so doing, they threw Eve under the bus—again—turning reasonable adult women who sought abortion into victims, awash in their own sad luck and bad judgment. Even Hillary Rodham Clinton turned back progress and contributed to this very public devaluing of women's choices. "We can all recognize that abortion in many ways represents a sad, even tragic choice to many, many women," she told an audience in 2005. (She has since revised her rhetoric, pushing back against the laws designed to erode women's choice: "Everything I have seen," she said during her 2016 campaign for president, "has convinced me that life is freer, fairer, healthier, safer, and far more humane when women are empowered to make their own reproductive health decisions.")

Imagining that they were building "common ground" with social conservatives, Democrats began to talk about "a third way," using language that cast abortion as morally difficult and the women who sought them as agonized, fretful, and full of pain. "Abortion is bad, and the ideal number of abortions is zero," wrote the pro-choice columnist Will Saletan in a *New York Times* op-ed. This strategy completely ignored the historical facts: as long as women have been getting pregnant, they have searched for ways to become un-pregnant, and for thousands of years, the methods they found were harmful to their health, causing infection, illness, and even death. And as a political maneuver, it backfired in incalculable ways, for all of a sudden a bipartisan moral consensus seemed to be emerging: if abortion is bad, then the women seeking abortion must also be bad, and new laws must be enacted to protect them from themselves.

The plight of women in Mississippi was also intensified by the ability of the nation's progressives and elites to look away from them, to disassociate themselves from their southern sisters or to regard them as beyond help. Before I took my trip down there, I too was guilty of believing that there was something "backward" about the state that justifies disengagement. Just as groups of people like to subordinate other groups of people to themselves and so obliterate their humanity, whole regions have been dehumanized as well. And Mississippi is the bottom of the bottom. Even people who hold ideals about equity and justice can find themselves thinking that the problems in Mississippi are too intransigent, so impossible to solve that no right-minded, forward-thinking person could ever hope to interact with them and find any success. And so the people of Mississippi become isolated in their suffering, cut off from a larger political and social world. This disdain for places like Mississippi is what allows its own non-democratic state government to persist. In a state that's 55 percent black, nearly every legislator in the state assembly is white.

Who enables the desperate isolation of the women of Mississippi? In part, it's liberal women with children who themselves became enraptured with the sonogram images they saw at the obstetrician's office and who wept when they heard the fetal heartbeat. Especially when I travel in upscale, liberal circles I see a fetishization of motherhood and children that I don't quite understand, a universe away from the hardscrabble world in which I grew up. This sacralization of motherhood in every sector of the privileged classes enables a widespread social conservatism that, at base, diminishes women's liberty: a consensus that motherhood is a woman's most important role. When a society tacitly agrees that a morally neutral, biological process—procreation—is "miraculous," then any intervention in that process can be seen as desecrating, and any choice against motherhood will be met with widespread disapproval. (In the churches I come from, a "miracle" is God's intervention in the natural order of things—an ability, say, to turn a flask of water into wine or one loaf of bread into many. The way I see it, through a doctor's eyes, there is perhaps nothing on earth less miraculous or more ordinary than the animal process of human procreation, which was happening long before the Bible was written and will continue long after today's newborns are dead.) But among the elites, the same people who write checks to Planned Parenthood, the whole enterprise of parenthood has taken on a hothouse aspect, which allows a blurry consensus about the "sanctity of life" to flourish—instead of a clear-eyed definition of what "life" really is. Mommy blogs, conversations about "having it all" and "helicopter parenting"—all contribute to a cultural neurosis around motherhood that obscures what ought to be a value-free choice. A cultish preference for motherhood is so embedded in culture that even well-meaning women reflexively judge one another for their reproductive choices. Now a "broad-minded" woman may be heard to disapprove out loud of her sister-in-law's abortion ("She could afford another baby!"), or to privately judge her friend's decision not to have children as "selfish." The truth is that there is no intrinsic moral value to becoming a mother or not becoming one. A woman who pursues a pregnancy is merely prioritizing her life around motherhood. And a woman who has an abortion is prioritizing her life around not wanting to become a mother or around devoting herself and her resources to the children she already has. *Homo sapiens* will continue to reproduce and evolve, with or without any individual woman's participation in that process.

But in Bible Belt states, the antis seized this widespread cultural reverence for motherhood as an opening. If a culture presumes that motherhood is, a priori, always a higher moral or even religious good, then people don't automatically revolt when laws are enacted that essentially force women into becoming mothers. Liberals may hear about laws enacted elsewhere, in states where they are not likely to live, that require counseling and waiting periods, widened hallways and hospital admitting privileges, and shrug: None of these seem, on the face of it, so bad. Shouldn't women be protected after all? But this is paternalism and complacency, a turning away from truth. As the late-night comedian and political commenta-

tor John Oliver puts it, "Abortion cannot be theoretically legal." It
will not matter that abortion is the law of the land if fewer and
fewer brick-and-mortar abortion clinics exist—shut down for lack
of compliance to a million new arbitrary rules and restrictions. Increasingly, limited or no access to abortion is a reality. Eighty-nine
percent of U.S. counties have no abortion provider at all; nearly
40 percent of American women of reproductive age live in these
counties. That means on average, a woman has to drive thirty miles
to a clinic, more than fifty if she lives in a rural area—and more if
she seeks an abortion after twenty weeks.

From the relative safety of the blue states, voters who support
abortion rights can be insulated from the devastating impact some
of the new laws make on women's lives. As governor of Indiana, Vice
President Mike Pence signed into law a bill that bans abortion on
the basis of a diagnosed fetal disability, and requires abortion providers to advise patients about perinatal hospice, in the event of a
lethal fetal anomaly. Perinatal hospice is not an established medical
protocol but a bundle of services invented by anti-abortion forces.
What the antis want is for nonviable fetuses to live inside the uterus
until they die of natural causes, which increases the risk of harm to
the health of the mother, because every pregnancy becomes more
potentially dangerous as it progresses to term. This same Indiana
law is the one that requires a miscarried or aborted fetus to be buried or cremated—even against a woman's wishes. In Alabama, a
2014 law requires a minor who wants an abortion without her parents' permission to go to court, where the state can appoint a lawyer for the fetus. The judge in charge can delay or adjourn the case
indefinitely, in effect causing the girl to "time out" of the legal abortion period, which in Alabama is twenty weeks post-fertilization. In

recent years, three states—Arizona, Arkansas, and South Dakota—passed laws requiring abortion providers to tell women who choose medication abortion that they can "reverse" the procedure by taking high doses of progesterone. This is, simply put, not true.

I implore all American women to examine their biases about abortion, to search their souls for the terrible double standard that defines this debate. Do you privately think that the poor women and women of color who live in regions far away are beyond your help or are, in some way, "not like" you? Do you perpetuate a bias by thinking that limiting access to abortion is okay for other (poor, black and Latina, or red state) women, as long as your private physician will prescribe the abortion pill for you if you need it, and as long as abortion clinics stay open in your state? Or are you secretly squeamish about abortion rights now that you've seen the sonogram images of your precious and beloved children in utero? Do you find yourself agreeing, a little, that life might begin at conception, that abortion is tragic? Do you think that if the women sitting in the chairs in the clinic only knew how gratifying motherhood is, they might reconsider?

Life is a process. Your life is a process. As a free human being, you are allowed to change your mind, to find yourself in different circumstances, to make mistakes. You are allowed to want your own future. What I see is this: The women who enter abortion clinic waiting rooms in states like Alabama and Mississippi are in possession of a resourcefulness and a resiliency that is impossible to see from the provinces in Los Angeles or Chicago or New York, and a pragmatic ability to reconcile what they understand about God with the very real circumstances of their lives. These women are no different from any women, anywhere. They are wise and intelligent.

They are more likely to have their hopes and dreams stifled, but they want the same things that anyone wants—namely, a feeling of control over the rest of their lives.

Working in the South brought this point home. When it comes to protecting the right to safe and legal abortion, all women are sisters. A legal threat to abortion access for a poor, African American woman is a legal threat to a white woman, too. A statewide ban on twenty-week abortions affects every woman, no matter what her income or where her kids go to school. It may be easy to look away from the plights of women like those who come to the clinics where I work, but if lawmakers succeed in stripping away the rights of poor women to obtain abortions, they will also be quietly but inexorably stripping away all women's rights. Solidarity is the best defense.

I have seen this solidarity at work, especially in recovery rooms. After abortions, women are frequently volatile, awash with relief or tearful at the end of a long inner journey. Frequently I have seen two women, virtual strangers, black and white, holding hands across their bed rails, one woman in the midst of her emotional turbulence and the other one helping her through it.

CHAPTER 11

Homecoming

I started doing abortions in my home state of Alabama even before I started working in Mississippi. More than other states, Mississippi has a rigid and punitive licensing procedure. I had to travel to Jackson to get fingerprinted before I could practice there, and it took a while for my license to come through. In the meantime, Diane needed help at the New Woman All Women clinic in Birmingham, the same clinic that was bombed in 1998 by Eric Rudolph, an incident in which a security officer was killed. When I showed up for work on my first day at the New Woman clinic, I was met by Emily Lyons, now sixty, the nurse who lost her eye and part of her hand in that bombing. She humbled me. At every phase of my post-conversion career, I had been forced to carefully consider the risks that I was undertaking, personally, by agreeing to do this work. The more invested I became in the cause of reproductive rights for women, the more I understood that I was putting myself on the line. And though I like to think of myself as brave, here was a woman who was truly heroic. She had lost half of her face, and half of one hand, and was nearly blind in her remaining eye. Yet she was still counseling women and protecting their rights.

In some ways, I had never left Alabama. I was always home for Christmas or Thanksgiving and found myself traveling there one or two more other times during the year. In addition, my brothers and sisters and I remained in close touch. But as I matured, I had begun to see myself not only as what I started out as, a black Southerner, but as what I had also become—a citizen of the world—comfortable with people of different races and cultures, a lover of travel, music, and food. Thrust back in Birmingham in this regular, routine way, I was forced to reconsider the city of my youth. Motivated now by reproductive justice concerns, I began to read voraciously about Birmingham's proud history in the struggle for civil rights. I inhaled Douglas Blackmon's book *Slavery by Another Name*, about Birmingham's role in the industrialization of our nation, moving from a large-scale agricultural economy, built on the backs of African slaves, to an economy based on steel and coal, built on the backs of black men who worked as indentured servants or who were forced to work as prison laborers serving indefinite terms. I read Diane McWhorter's staggering work *Carry Me Home*, about the activism and terrorism that defined Birmingham in the 1960s. I learned that during the civil rights struggle, Birmingham was known as Bombingham, a reference to the regular domestic terrorism inflicted on blacks. I delved into the life of Reverend Fred Shuttlesworth, a Birmingham native, cofounder of the Southern Christian Leadership Conference and a colleague of King, who helped orchestrate the Freedom Rides. According to legend, when beaten nearly to death by the Ku Klux Klan, Shuttlesworth told a police officer that "I wasn't raised to run."

Certainly, the stories of these civil rights heroes clarified for me the danger I face, but also instilled in me a tranquility about my life's work. I will never forget my first visit to the 16th Street Baptist Church. It was bombed when I was less than one year old, and though it was reconstructed almost immediately, I didn't visit until I was fifty-one. Today, the church is a regular stop on civil rights pilgrimages, with tour buses frequently parked at its curb. Tourists take photos of the rose window, installed after the bombing, depicting a black Jesus in glass, and they shudder when they descend to the basement and see the clock there, preserved from the bombing, which stopped telling time at 10:22.

Four young girls were assassinated that day: Addie Mae Collins, Carol Denise McNair, Carole Robertson, and Cynthia Wesley. The oldest of these was fourteen years old. For me, it's meaningful and symbolic that the victims of the violence that day were female. They had their lives—their potential to grow into women—taken away. The analogies are clear. The women who come to abortion clinics in the South are being denied control of their bodies and their lives.

In January 2012, three months before my Mississippi licensure came through, the people had elected a new Republican governor, Phil Bryant, who had vowed to make Mississippi an abortion-free state. Then, in April, he signed into law a bill (similar to the Texas law, ruled unconstitutional by the Supreme Court in 2016) that required all the physicians working at Jackson Women's Health to be board-certified ob-gyns, and more: we had to obtain admitting privileges from a local hospital in order, the bill's sponsors insisted, to protect the "health and safety" of the women of Mississippi in the event of mishap during the surgical procedure. Now everyone on every side understood that this "health and safety" rationale was ridiculously bogus: the real intent of the law was to shut the clinic down. Abortion is safer than outpatient plastic surgery and many other procedures—and those doctors are not required to have admitting privileges. What's more, the 0.05 percent of patients who need to be admitted to the hospital because of an accident or incident occurring during an abortion would be admitted through the hospital emergency department, no special "privileges" required. These laws were designed to entrap doctors like me, coming from out of town with no local connections, and from the moment I started performing abortions in Mississippi, I found myself ensnared in their web. I had a medical degree from the University of Iowa, a public health degree from Harvard. I had held faculty appointments at the University of Hawaii, as well as Howard and Northwestern Universities. But I could not get hospital admitting privileges in Jackson, Mississippi, because no one in town would break ranks and give them to me. It was a catch-22. In July, the health department in Jackson threatened to shut the clinic down for noncompliance with the law.

That's when the Center for Reproductive Rights stepped in. CRR is a New York City–based advocacy group, a collection of lawyers who observe the nation's legal landscape around abortion rights and take on cases they believe will have the biggest impact. They represented my friend Amy Hagstrom Miller and Whole Woman's Health in their victorious 2016 Supreme Court case against the state of Texas. They are warriors, pushing back against the tide of laws that restrict access. And Nancy Northrup, who runs CRR, believed that the Mississippi law was unconstitutional—for without a single abortion clinic in the entire state of Mississippi, women would be deprived of their constitutional right to a safe and legal abortion, as provided by *Roe*. As CRR prepared to file suit in federal court, its lawyers asked me if I would agree to be named, in court documents, as a plaintiff, along with the clinic itself. The way I felt about the thing was this. If I am not willing to stand up—in public, with my face on the news—and advocate for women, then where were the guts of my commitment? If I am willing to put myself physically in harm's way but don't do what it takes to protect access to abortion and to build capacity by keeping clinics open and encouraging more physicians to perform abortions by inspiring them with my example, then what have I changed my life for? I didn't mind the public scrutiny. I knew that my credentials were unassailable: no one could find anything wrong with my practice. More, I have no one I am obligated to protect—except for the women who depend on me every day, to give them what they need in a skillful and compassionate way. It was as if God had put me in Mississippi to stand up for women. The only real answer for me was "Yes."

I always saw my family when I passed through, but never told them, exactly, what I was doing there. They knew, of course, that I was a doctor and that I had made good on my mother's constant prediction, that I was a "smart boy." They were proud of me. That was good enough for them, and they never asked any questions.

But around the time I became a plaintiff in the clinic's lawsuit against the state of Mississippi, my baby brother, Steve, got sick, a lethal combination of hypertension and cardiovascular and pulmonary disease. Unable to work, he lost his job as a laborer at a steel plant. Without a job, he was unable to keep up with the payments on the car he had recently bought. I was living in D.C. at the time and commuting to Alabama and Mississippi. Wanting to help my brother out of a tight spot, I phoned Steve and told him that if he could travel to Washington to pick it up, I would give him my car, a Honda I rarely used. He and his wife came to see me in May 2012, and when I saw Steve for the first time since the prior Thanksgiving, I was shocked. A better word might be heartbroken. I knew he was sick, but I was not prepared for the extent to which he had decompensated. He weighed nearly five hundred pounds. He was sweating profusely. Any small exertion, such as walking up the stairs to my apartment, made him short of breath, and his lack of air was making him desperate and anxious. When I saw him through my doctor's eyes, I realized that Steve might die.

It took another year or so for my life to resolve itself in a way that allowed me to move back to Birmingham full-time, but it was during that visit that I understood what I needed to do. Steve's health was so fragile. As a physician, I knew I could help manage his care, and help guide him through the health-care system. As his older brother, and the closest thing to a father that he ever had, I wanted to keep an eye on him. More than that: I wanted to be a positive influence, provide an uplift to his mood. I wanted to help him, if I could, stand by him in solidarity, and encourage him to lose some weight and stop smoking and drinking. (Smoking he stopped immediately, as for drinking, he still enjoys a social shot of Hennessy, or "Henny" as he calls it, from time to time. Sometimes the antis make me wish I drank, which would allow me to have a shot with Steve and Fred when we brothers get together!) I hoped that Steve might learn again to embrace life, and not sit around in his house, refusing to move, afraid that his life was over.

So for personal as well as professional reasons, the idea of moving back home resonated with me. Even though I was, in some ways, a fish out of water in Birmingham, an African American abortion provider born into poverty in this self-same city, I had begun to feel comfortable with my new reality. I found blessings in my achievement, and I liked that I was both insider and outsider at once. This was my home. I belonged here, and yet I was also a stranger. I began to glimpse how my life trajectory and my unique identity might empower others to do this work and bring attention to the lack of access. I hoped that by putting down stakes in Birmingham, at least for a time, I might inspire other abortion providers to regard the South not just as a battleground, or a place where poor people needed their help, but as a place where progressive-minded physicians might comfortably live, setting an example for their peers. Advocacy is that much more meaningful when you live within the community you're serving—and not just flying in and out, blind to and disconnected from all the adjacent problems of racism, poverty, and a dimming of dreams. I found myself at a point in life where I wanted to model that level of commitment. So I rented a small apartment in a gentrifying area of Birmingham. A documentary filmmaker lived right above me and a bass player lived next door. I put my collection of cooking pans in the kitchen and my double bass in a corner of the living room, and limited my circuit to the South. I worked in Tuscaloosa, Montgomery, and Jackson, traveling occasionally to Atlanta, to the Women's Center in Buckhead.

My siblings found out that I am an abortion doctor because I started appearing on television. My first major appearance, I remember, was on Sunday, July 1, 2012, just after CRR filed its lawsuit against the state of Mississippi, and I was invited onto MSNBC to talk to Melissa Harris-Perry about it. Steve saw me on television and was surprised as anything. Word quickly spread among my family. I don't think I was avoiding the subject. I think it just didn't seem important—my relationships with my siblings are based in blood and kinship, not circumstance. We, like so many families, have been through a lot. We've experienced loss, divorce, single-parenthood, drug addiction, health problems, and jail—and none of my siblings have ever felt the need to call another out or criticize individual choices. I had never felt that I needed to make an official announcement to my family about my profession, and it turns out that I was right. None of my siblings has any objection in principle to what I do for a living, and all of them are as proud as can be. When they called me up later to razz me about my encounter with Harris-Perry on national television, they didn't mention abortion, or lawsuits, or the controversy my professional choices were bound to stir up. What they said was how much I resembled our mother. I had, they told me with love, "that Parker smirk."

CHAPTER 12

Ethical Abortion Care

One day, a twelve-year-old girl was sitting in the waiting room in Tuscaloosa with her mother. She was caramel complected and physically mature, but with the face of a child. When she came in that morning she had been shy and silent, but she had been given a Xanax, the same as all the other patients, and now she was sitting there among a bunch of other women a lot older than her, feeling voluble and disinhibited. When her mother went outside to the parking lot for a smoke, one of the other patients, a white woman who happened to have a twelve-year-old daughter at home, turned to her and gently struck up a conversation, hoping in a maternal way to guide her away from what she imagined was inappropriate contact with older boys at school. "Who were you messing with?" she asked the girl. "Don't you know not to go around with those boys?"

The girl replied, so naively that she was almost sassy, "He isn't a boy. He's fifty-three and he's my daddy, and after this he's going to pick us up and go get ice cream." The waiting room went silent. And then the white woman got up from her chair and made her way past all the knees and crossed ankles and hands in laps, and through the swinging doors that led to the procedure rooms and down the long hallway to the owner's office. By the time the girl's mother came inside, we had taken the girl into a back office. Gloria Gray, the clinic's owner, had called child protective services and the police were on their way. Gloria and I were in complete agreement about our mandated duty to report situations of this type to authorities, an obligation that I honor with all dependent minors. But when the mother didn't see her daughter in the waiting room, she immediately became suspicious. The situation became dramatic.

The antis like to paint us, the physicians who provide abortion care, as emotional automatons, like car mechanics performing abortions on customers for a fee. "Abortion on demand," the antis' phrase, contains all these meanings. To the antis, a commitment to "choice" is an unthinking, unexamined thing—as reductive and simplistic as "life begins at conception." But a passionate commitment to women's agency and self-determination does not exclude an ethical framework, and over the years I have worked hard to develop a complex and three-dimensional sense of the morality around what being an abortion provider means. I have worked out my own ethics around the issue, and I hold them firmly while being open to change. And, truth be told, calling CPS that day was one of the hardest things I have ever had to do. This girl had been adopted by these parents out of foster care and had been living with them for six years. She was grateful to and protective of the people whom she saw as her family. She did not fully understand the inappropriateness of her father having sex with her. "He doesn't do it anymore," she told the social worker who arrived with the police. And the mother, too, was in denial, believing that if she kept close enough tabs on her husband, her daughter would be safe from him. The girl's reality was a heartbreaking one. But based on where I come from, and on my two dozen years providing health care for women, I know that moving a twelve-year-old girl from one foster home to another does nothing to improve her chances in life. This girl was stuck between two terrible places.

I become enraged when I think of the men who do this kind of thing, who rob girls of their childhoods and violate their trust simply to satisfy their own sexual urges. But in my years of doing this work, I have come to understand that how I feel about each individual patient has to be set aside in the procedure room, or at least subjugated to a more rationalistic, conscientious, ethical mind-set. I cannot let my own emotions and impulses inform my actions. My work cannot depend on whether I like a patient or dislike her, whether I approve of her circumstances or disapprove. I rarely intervene in patients' lives. For if I take my Christian commitment not to judge women seriously—and I do, more seriously than anything—then I first must concede that I am human, a person with my own deeply held biases, rooted in how and where I was raised and the trajectory of my life. In order not to act on those biases or to impose them on other people, I have developed a clear ethical framework that I apply to providing abortion care in every case, which I hope allows me to push personal judgments aside. This framework allows me to see the humanity in every woman and also provides me a space in which I do my job efficiently, compassionately, and well.

First, I obey the law. This means calling child protective services when a minor comes to one of the clinics where I work and intentionally or unintentionally makes a charge of incest or abuse. My own rage at the people whom the state entrusted to care for her, and my knowledge of public health and the prospects for children who are abused or shuttled around from home to home, who are impeded as children from ever establishing bonds of trust, must be put aside. I do what the law requires me to do. I did not perform the girl's abortion on the day she was in the Tuscaloosa clinic, and she went home with a social worker to be placed into a new foster home—and not with her mother, whom she loved and to whom she felt a strong familial connection. I did give her a D&E four weeks later, in a clinic in Atlanta, where we had the ability to sedate her completely. Then we sent the fetal tissue back to Alabama with an officer of the court, where it would be DNA-tested and used as evidence against her adoptive father.

In keeping with my commitment to abide by the law, I also comply with every TRAP regulation, no matter how unjust or discriminatory I believe it to be. I do this because it's more important to me to provide abortions than to not provide them, and because I understand that my reputation for being an excellent provider of "safe and legal" abortion is all I have; the minute I resort to guerrilla tactics, I have given away the high ground.

In my work, I abide by the consensus, established by *Roe* and by medical science, around "viability." According to *Roe*, the state has a compelling interest to protect the life of a fetus only when it reaches the point where it can survive outside the womb with the aid of medical technology. I will not terminate a pregnancy beyond twenty-five weeks. For a million reasons, this boundary makes sense to me. For one thing, although abortion is very safe, it gets riskier as the gestational age of the fetus increases. I don't feel comfortable assuming that risk—especially if a woman's only rationale for wanting to terminate is her personal preference. I won't do it. If you're twenty-eight weeks and you just don't want to be pregnant, or you just don't want to give birth—that's not an appropriate use of my skills.

But I don't believe in moral absolutes, and so even this ethical refusal has a wrinkle. In keeping with my insistence that women be the agents of their own lives and futures, I will refer a woman who wants an abortion at twenty-five weeks to another doctor. There are three outpatient clinics in the United States (in Colorado, New Mexico, and Maryland) that do third-trimester abortions, almost always in the case of a fatal fetal anomaly or a risk of life to the mother. A young woman once came to the Tuscaloosa clinic with her mother. She said she thought she was eight or ten weeks along, but the minute I put my hand on her belly I knew she was much further than that. Maybe she was lying to me because she had lied to her mother. Maybe she had lied to herself. I don't know. But when I did her sonogram, I saw that she was twenty-eight weeks pregnant—long past the Alabama ban at twenty weeks (post-fertilization), past the line of viability, past my medical expertise and my ethical comfort zone. "Is there anyplace she can get an abortion?" the mother pleaded. I gave them contact information for the clinics in Colorado and New Mexico and told them that an abortion in those places costs between $7,000 and $15,000. I did not tell them that the doctors in those places would probably not perform the procedure because, at twenty-eight weeks, patient preference—or "I messed up"—is not a medical indication. It is not my role to block anyone from pursuing their interest or to withhold information.

I also refuse to perform abortions on women who I believe are being coerced. So many different factors play into a woman's decision that this can be hard to discern. Every kind of woman winds up on my table, and I don't interrogate the circumstances of their lives, because personal details are outside my purview. I don't need to know who they were with or why or whether they're cheating or how horny they were or how sorry they are, and this boundary helps me maintain my stance of total compassion and lack of judgment. The women on my table are married or single or having sex with multiple partners. They can be fifteen years old or forty-five, rich or on welfare, employed or not, thin or obese, gorgeous or plain. As I like to put it, every kind of woman ends up in jacked-up situations; my job is, very simply, to help them out. But at the same time, I do everything I can to explore what for me is the central question, which has two parts. First: Have you made this decision yourself? And second: Are you resolved about it? A woman is entitled to her own regret, as well as her own inner conflict and moral ambivalence. But I will not do an abortion if I sense that it is not her own desire.

Internal conflict about abortion is entirely normal. I would even say it's the usual path. Many of the women I see would like to bring their pregnancy to term but feel that they can't. A woman with five children just lost her youngest one to cancer and doesn't have the emotional bandwidth. A woman with three children just got divorced and her youngest child hasn't learned to walk. A woman just lost her job—and her income and her health insurance. A woman is sick, or her mother is sick, or she wishes her boyfriend would stick around but he won't. I define a dilemma as a decision between two undesirable options with no opportunity to avoid the choice. The vast majority of the women I see have navigated their dilemma and have landed firmly in the place in which they find themselves that they are. The specifics of their decision path are immaterial to me. My job is to probe for a lack of resolve, for that's where the ethical danger zones lie.

Coercion comes in many forms, and over the years, I have seen it play out in myriad ways. When I was a young doctor, I developed an interest in intimate-partner abuse—the first cause I became involved in as an activist. I was at Harvard, in my thirties, working on my public health degree, and I saw a film about domestic violence and the ways in which abusers cover their tracks. And I flashed back in a tingling, gut-wrenching moment to a patient I saw my first year out of residency when I was in Merced, California. A white woman, in her thirties, came into the clinic where I worked complaining of generalized pelvic pain. I took her history, and the whole time her husband never left her side. As I asked her questions, he chimed in constantly—always sweet and doting but never letting her answer for herself. And when it was time to do the pelvic exam, he even accompanied her into the examining room. "Honey," he said in his sweet voice, "I want to be there with you. I don't want you to go through this alone." That day at Harvard I learned that 30 percent of women who see their doctors for generalized pelvic pain are victims of abuse or rape, and I remembered how the wife smiled at me—with her face but not her eyes. I did not know enough that day in Merced—and I missed all the signs—and I sent the woman home with some pain medication and told her to come back in a couple weeks. I never saw her again. I will regret it for the rest of my life.

In the abortion clinics where I work, I make it a point to investigate every bruise I see on a woman on the examining table. Sometimes a woman can get a bruise on her inner thigh from bumping a table—but not usually. And when I do investigate, a woman will frequently say she's decided to terminate the pregnancy in order to escape an abusive partner; she knows full well that having a child will bind her to her abuser for the rest of her life. But sometimes the balance swings the other way, and the woman is on my table because someone—a boyfriend, a father, a mother—is forcing her to be there. I have become adept at discerning these cases, too, which usually cross my radar because of a woman's tears. When I ask her about the tears, she says, "My boyfriend says if I don't have this abortion, he's going to . . ." do something. Beat her. Kill her. Leave her. Kill her children or her mother. No matter what I'm doing, I stop right there. This happened, most memorably, when I was working at Planned Parenthood in Washington, D.C. I had a patient who was about twenty-seven years old, engaged to be married. She had been holding it together through the sonogram and the prep, but as soon as I put the speculum in, she started to cry uncontrollably. When I queried this flood of emotion, she told me that her fiancé said that if she didn't have the abortion, he would leave her. At that point, I stopped what I was doing. I removed the speculum. I hear what you are saying, I said. But I can't do this unless I know this decision is coming from you. She could not stop crying, so I got her up from the table and sent her back to the lockers to put her clothes on and to have another conversation with a counselor. If after counseling you are resolute, I will perform your abortion, I told her. She left the clinic and she never came back.

When a woman tells me that her boyfriend has threatened to kill her or beat her if she does not terminate, I will refuse to perform her abortion. I have no reason to disbelieve you, I will say. But this is a legal problem, and I am a doctor, not a lawyer and not a police officer. We will help you get into a shelter. We will help you get a restraining order against your boyfriend. If, after you get yourself away from your boyfriend, you find that terminating the pregnancy is something that you want to do, well then, I am here next Wednesday through Friday and the clinic opens at seven in the morning.

It pains me to say this, but sometimes mothers—who believe they're being caring and have their daughters' best interests at heart—are the worst. When I see teenage patients sitting with hovering mothers in the waiting room, I pay close attention. And before the girl gets on the table, I will separate her from her mother and bring her into an empty examination room while she's still got her sweatpants on. In these cases, I look the young woman straight in the eye, and ask, "Do you want to have this abortion?"

Sometimes the girl says yes, and we can proceed. But frequently she says no. *My mother wants me to.* And then I have to send her back to the waiting room to talk with her mother. Oftentimes, there's shouting. Often, the mother will say to her daughter, *Unless you have this abortion, you can't come home with me.* And then she'll approach me, with steam and smoke coming out of her ears and eyes, saying, *What have you done! I am her mother. I've already paid. I want my money back!*

I am outwardly cool, and more than that: I am sure of what my job is and what it isn't. I do not perform abortions on women who don't want them. If a mother is threatening to withhold support, or love, or shelter from her pregnant daughter, I will make sure the girl understands what that means for her. *It's good for you to know now that if you want to carry this pregnancy forward, you won't have your mother's support. If you want to have this baby, we can figure out ways to get you help. We can help you find a place to live. But it's good for you to know early on that you're on your own.* By framing the girl's reality in these terms, she may see her situation differently. She may consider, realistically, how it will be to raise a child on her own as a teenager and she may come to a different decision. Or she may not.

If the mother and the daughter are in a more conciliatory place, I or the counselors working in the clinic will try to mediate. I remember a time in Montgomery, when a seventeen-year-old girl, who was eight weeks pregnant, indicated to me that she didn't want the abortion, her mother did. When I sent her back to the waiting room, both mother and daughter burst into tears. I approached them both. Today is not your day, I said. You all need to talk, and you don't need to do it right here, or right now. You have some time. And then I turned to the mother: But please know that when your daughter comes back, I'm going to ask her the exact same questions that I did today, and unless she can get through them honestly and tell me that this is what she wants, I'm not going perform her abortion. I have to believe that this is her decision, and I can sense when people are faking or have rehearsed their answers. This is the only ethical context in which I can be an abortion provider.

Discerning a woman's true intent is usually easy. But not always. Women who come to an abortion clinic seeking to terminate a pregnancy are frequently in an amplified emotional state. They can be pensive. They can be angry. They can be anxious. No woman entering an abortion clinic ever says, to me or to her mother or to anyone, "Oh, happy day! I'm going to have an abortion!" But if a woman is crying, I make it my business always to ask. I always say, "Tell me what the tears are about." And if she says, "No, I'm fine," I insist. "Tell me. Because people who are crying aren't usually 'fine.'" A woman can be conflicted and certain at the same time, and my duty, my responsibility, to the patient and to myself is to make sure that's all it is. I never say, "Do you want an abortion?"—because an abortion is never anything a woman actively wants. I say, "Are you sure?" I need to be able to trust my patients and take them at their word, so that even if *they* have regret, *I* won't have any.

There was one time in my entire career when I understood, clearly and in hindsight, that I had performed an abortion on a woman who did not want one, and the memory of that incident still floods me with helplessness and rage. Again, this was at Planned Parenthood in Washington, D.C. The patient was a very observant Muslim woman who had come to the clinic with her husband. The man was calling all the shots. He came in insisting, for religious reasons, that a female doctor perform the procedure. And when he discovered that I was their only choice—I was the doctor working in the clinic that day—he arranged for me to do the procedure, but asked that I agree with certain conditions. I would not talk with the patient, or ask her any questions, or look her in the eye. The staff, in an effort to be culturally sensitive, always took multiple measures to overcome language and cultural barriers, and I trusted them. Out of respect for the couple's cultural background, I agreed. And after the procedure was over, I looked at the woman's face for the first time, and she was crying. And she said, in broken English, "I never wanted to do this." I believe that I have never been so angry. In this one incident, my hands were tied, or I felt that they were, and now I have to live with my regret.

Another thing I will not do: I will not give an abortion to a woman who is expressing child preference, who prefers to have a boy rather than a girl, or a white child rather than a black child. Even in America, in the twenty-first century, this can and does occur. Many of my patients come from conservative religious or cultural backgrounds, and while I feel that it is my job to be respectful of the decision making of other people based on all kinds of factors, I do not exercise that respect at the expense of my own moral convictions. So if a woman says to me, this fetus is female, and if I don't have a son I will be beaten, I won't do her abortion. Just as I would refuse to do an abortion for a woman who tells me she's sleeping with a Jewish man and her family would never accept a

Jewish baby. I refuse to get engaged with stereotyping or profiling. I don't think of the world in terms of good and evil, but as Dr. King said, "Non-cooperation with evil is as much a moral obligation as is cooperation with good." The stigmatization of females—or of anyone—is not acceptable to me.

In the abortion clinics where I work, I try to cultivate compassion—not just in myself, but among the staff and even among the patients themselves, who meet in my waiting rooms having come from all different walks of life and whose pregnancies and abortion decisions mean something different to each one. I have zero tolerance for women who judge one another or who presume that their abortion, and their circumstances, are somehow more stressful or more extenuating than anyone else's. I remember a lawyer who came to see me in Montgomery. She was well educated and charismatic. But as she lay on the table, she began to complain about the irreverent jokes and wisecracks that the other patients were making as they sat, stressing, in the waiting room, drinking soda and eating chips. She said, "Don't they know that this is very difficult for some of us? Can't they show some respect?" And though I didn't show it, I got angry, because no one is entitled to sit in judgment of others, no matter their education, their status, their station, the circumstances that led them through our doors. She wanted her abortion to be sacred, and more, she wanted others to express their feelings in a way that was compatible with her sensibility. Well, all of this—the procedure, every woman in the waiting room, the nurses and aids and administrators who provide this excellent care, my own hard-won skill—is sacred to me. When she wrote a letter to complain of the atmosphere in our clinic, I was unmoved.

CHAPTER 13

A New Theology of Abortion

When I lived in Hawaii, I joined a Quaker meeting. The meetinghouse was a home in a residential neighborhood in Manoa Valley, a place with groomed lawns and a constant view of the mountain. I was in recovery, as I like to say, from organized religion. During my medical training, I seldom went to church. And in California, where I had lived prior to moving to Honolulu, I found that I preferred working at a food bank across the street from a church on Sundays than going to the church itself. The idea of Quakerism had always appealed to me. I liked its social justice history, its activism in the abolition and civil rights movements. And I liked its radical democracy. In Quakerism, there is no formal doctrine or creed, except a commitment to nonviolence and a belief that every individual on earth possesses a divine inner light. In a Quaker meeting, no one is in charge. There are no clergy. There is no liturgy, no hymns, and no altar. The meeting begins, and people sit quietly, in silence, with their own thoughts, in a circle. If a truth rises within someone, then sometimes that person will speak what's within his or her heart. But mostly, a Quaker meeting is quiet.

Quakerism gave me the space I needed to experience God in a meditative, contemplative, highly personal way—and at the same time remain within a community of believers. I jokingly say that I'm born again from being born again. My time in Hawaii, in the middle of my life, gave me more than a professional, vocational clarity: it gave me the liberty to understand my faith in a fully humanistic way. If God is human and humans are of God, then God has to love everything about us, and we have to love all that belongs to God.

I have never doubted the truth of my Christian conversion, which I had that day in 1978, when I was fifteen years old. In that park, I asked Jesus into my heart and He came. I still sincerely believe that a transformative, mythical experience occurred for me that afternoon, and I am grateful for it. That moment, in a very authentic sense, gave me my future.

It wasn't long before some of the very rigid beliefs that accompanied the fundamentalism that I learned from Pastor Mike began to chafe at me, and as early as my freshman year at Berea, I entered a phase of questioning. How might I believe that God created the world, when I loved biology and knew about evolution? How might I hold the Bible's version of male dominance over women when my mother raised me better than any man? How might I square my church's repugnance for premarital sex with the fact that many good people I knew in the dorms were having sex with regularity? How might I think about slavery and justice and the very punitive terms the Bible sets for the faithful that violate God's rules? How might I think about hell? The black church in which I was raised gave me my life, but it also, I began to see, preserved taboos around subjects where there should have been relief: not just about abortion but also homosexuality and sexual abuse. I have come to understand that the entrenchment of patriarchal authority and power—even in the black church—has allowed women who sit in the pews to experience shame and rejection around their sexuality. It has vilified gay men and made lesbians invisible. For too many people, God has ceased to be present in the very place that He should live.

In college, I peeked my head out of the insular world in which I had grown up and started to read beyond my Bible. At Berea, when I was nineteen years old, I read *Letter from Birmingham Jail* and *The Autobiography of Malcolm X*. I saw in Dr. King, especially, a path forward. He maintained his deep, deep roots in his faith tradition, and at the same time embodied an intellectual rigor that was so attractive to me. He was philosophical, thoughtful, *and* Christian. He was an activist. I read Dr. King and then I read the books Dr. King had read, the twentieth-century theologians who built a progressive Christianity that put God at the center of history and made justice God's priority: Reinhold Niebuhr and Paul Tillich, who led me to a more complex understanding about moral absolutes. I read their forebears, Hegel and Schleiermacher and Kierkegaard. It was as if I could feel my mind expanding—exploding—with each book. I began to understand that I had to find a thinking person's religion or abandon God entirely.

My mentor in this journey toward a broader understanding of Christian identity was another Mike, a former Roman Catholic priest named Mike Rivage-Seul. Mike was a professor at Berea who taught Issues & Values, that course I loved. It was he who suggested that I write about abortion in my paper, and he who, with great irony, complimented the gigantic pin I wore on my lapel that said

JESUS. Ordained around the time of the Second Vatican Council, a period of upheaval in the Church, Mike had left the priesthood and then fallen in love with a woman and married her—though his commitment to his faith stayed strong. And as his faith evolved, Mike became devoted to liberation theology, a rearticulation of the gospels' message on radical love for the poor and the marginalized. Whole swaths of the Roman Catholic Church were rebelling against the more hierarchal vision of Catholicism preached in so many parish churches and embracing this revolutionary, leftist vision, allying themselves especially with communists and the working poor in Latin America—against the dictatorial governments there and against the bourgeois authority of their own Church. And though I didn't know it at the time, groups of African American Protestant intellectuals were embracing liberation theology, too, and preaching it to their people in the form of prophetic sermons about upheaval and justice. The liberation theologians were leading a charge of antiauthoritarian righteousness in the name of Jesus. In Dr. King, in Mike, and the ideas he taught me, I could begin to see new versions of myself.

The Christianity I learned as a boy began to seem, as I continued to devour these ideas, shallow, emotional, and naive. I know that every serious faithful person goes through this, a dark period of questioning, and my twenties were that for me. How might I reconcile my ability to think critically, which was becoming a requirement as I pursued my path through science toward becoming a medical doctor, and at the same time continue to see myself as a person of deep faith? In my day-to-day college life, I was still hanging out with my friends from InterVarsity, the evangelical Christian student group on campus. I was still maintaining my stance of sexual abstinence and handing out tracts door-to-door, and when I went home to Birmingham I always saw Pastor Mike. These were the people with whom I felt comfortable, whom I loved, even as I began to lose my notion of moral absolutes and think more in terms of shades of gray. I didn't yet know where I was going to end up, but the more I read, the more I understood that I needed a God of transcendence and justice more than I needed one that enshrined and preserved the Bible's antique, patriarchal worldview. When I left Berea, I took with me a compliment paid by Mike Rivage-Seul, one I cherish to this day: "I admire your commitment to Christianity," he told me one day after class. "You hold your faith in an intelligent way."

Many seem to accept, without thinking, that to be a Christian is to oppose abortion rights. In my view, the only Christianity that mandates an anti-abortion view is an emotion-based faith—a rigid reading of Scripture that invites no questioning or interpretive consideration. The Bible is not stuck in time, but rather a living, breathing, divinely inspired document, and the God that I believe exists within its pages is big enough, and flexible enough, and loving enough to accommodate a very different perspective. More: my God is a radical God who requires us to love one another *because of our own sinfulness* and to be generous with one another even when our impulses want to lead us back to the safety of those childish, narrow beliefs that make us afraid to act.

I had no way of knowing this when I was young, when I was writing my paper on abortion for Issues & Values or querying the boundaries of my faith, but Christians have a long tradition of supporting abortion rights—in public and in the political sphere. Even before *Roe v. Wade*, progressive Christians and Jews have been preaching from the pulpit what the Reverend Tom Davis, a minister in the United Church of Christ, calls a "humane theology," a belief that a woman contemplating abortion deserves to be treated with compassion, and that her own judgment and experience must be trusted. Humane theology was the foundation of Dr. George Tiller's practice. It dictates that alleviating needless suffering is a Christian's sacred responsibility. If God is in everything, and everyone, then God is as much in the woman making a decision to terminate a pregnancy as in her Bible. "The sacred," writes Davis in his book *Sacred Work: Planned Parenthood and Its Clergy Alliances*, "is more often revealed not in abstract pronouncements, but in the experience of human beings trying to deal with the inequities and tragedies of human life."

These brave and righteous religious leaders for reproductive rights, warriors really, have been so widely ignored, for decades, by the public and the press. As far back as 1967, when abortion was still illegal in New York State, the Reverend Howard Moody, of Judson Memorial Church in New York City, formed the Clergy Consultation Service on Abortion—a kind of Underground Railroad coalition of Jewish and Christian clerics committed to helping women procure safe abortion care. They were motivated, Reverend Moody said, by their "humane concern" for the women who were forced to risk their lives navigating the underworld of illegal abortion on their own. Like the Good Samaritan, the ministers assumed the legal risk on behalf of women because their faith compelled them to provide succor to a population they saw as persecuted and vulnerable.

An estimated 450,000 women called on the Clergy Consultation Service for help in the six years before *Roe*—and the coalition, which started with twenty-one members, grew to two thousand.

Activism by Moody's group helped propel New York's legislature to legalize abortion in 1970, the first state in the nation to do so. Emboldened by it success, the Clergy Consultation Service then began to help women from other states travel to New York to obtain safe and legal abortions, and then, breaking with the medical establishment, these same clerics proposed the model for the first abortion clinic. Believing that women's privacy and autonomy would be better served if they could get their abortion care in a freestanding clinic instead of in a hospital, Moody's group worked with a doctor committed to providing "low cost, quality care, humane treatment and a willingness to serve the poor" in a freestanding place. Women's Services, on Manhattan's Upper East Side, was the first abortion clinic in the country.

Then, in 1973, when *Roe* came under attack by Catholic and conservative Christian groups, an activist Christian group rose up in opposition. The Religious Coalition for Reproductive Choice has fought tirelessly in the political sphere, arguing for "reproductive choice as a basic part of religious liberty," and maintaining that the availability of safe, legal abortion for anyone who needs it is the only compassionate course for women and families. RCRC has filed amicus briefs in major abortion cases. It fights personhood bills, which give equal legal rights to fetuses, and abortion bans. Its members include Catholics, Episcopalians, Lutherans, Unitarians, Methodists, Presbyterians, Jews, and Congregationalists. I am on the governing board of that organization. And still, its efforts can seem, to the public, nearly invisible.

For years, I was content to stay in my stuckness, to allow my mind and my faith to expand, but to let that evolution happen in private, on my own time. I was contented in my Quaker meeting.

Bigger, corporate expressions of faith held no attraction for me, and no traditional congregation could do the work of helping me understand myself to myself. And so, outwardly, I continued to say I was "born again," and on that basis to refuse to perform abortions with my own two hands.

Then, as circumstance forced me out of my complacency, professionally, so did it force me to articulate a new understanding of God, which would prompt, embrace, and support my professional choice. This understanding I came to on my own, with my books, and my tapes, and the voices of my loving mentors and personal saints in my head. And I reassert it here, in the hope that other Christians, and other people of faith, might find in my evolution some comfort— and perhaps some inspiration to see abortion as part God. Talking openly about abortion should be something that happens in church, and not suppressed by religious authorities in the interest of preserving their own power. Women should find healing and understanding in church, not stigma and shame.

The more I try to comprehend the notion of God, the more I think about the vastness of it. Thomas Merton said, "God *is*." Everything we can understand is within the reality of God. Because we're so limited, we have a tendency to anthropomorphize. God is a person. God is a man. In the West, God is a white man who runs everything. That is the limited understanding that I sought to escape. Merton used to say, "God is that which is wholly Other." God is not you, and God is not me, and God is not somebody or something else. Unless you can get beyond the animate and the personal—beyond anything we can describe—then you can't get to the goodness and the bigness of that which is Other. Everything, *everything*, transpires within that context. And so conception, life,

death, birth, abortion—they're all processes playing out in the reality of that Other. I don't have this truncated view that life begins
exactly here or ends exactly there. Static processes don't resonate
with my understanding of God.

To say that conception, or birth, or even death is "miraculous"
does an injustice to God. Only a person lacking a scientific understanding of reproduction would say that God gives life, or God takes
life, or you won't get pregnant unless God makes you pregnant. This
idea of God, as a meddler, is what allows the antis to turn faithful
people against themselves—because in their eyes, all decisions, all
the meaningful parts of life, are "God's will" or "not God's will." Is
God really that temperamental and petty? Does God really need all
that adoration? I'm thinking of the baseball player who comes up
to bat and does some comical praying, kissing thing with his hands
and on the visor of his cap before he hits a home run or strikes out,
swinging at the air. Does that have anything to do with God? Does
God really care about the outcome of a baseball game? Is God really
on one team's side? In this narrow view of God, there are good guys
and bad guys, and only God gets to decide.

If God is wholly Other, then the miracle of life is not some ordinary meeting of sperm and ovum—a morally neutral, purely
biological event—but the agency and the responsibility that come
with being able to participate with God in a creative process. God is
not human. God is not on the planet. God does not have babies, or
make babies. People do. As part of a greater intelligence, as a lover
of beauty and creativity, God made the world. And sexual reproduction is part of a collaborative process—between a male and a female
and between God and humans. In that process, all distinctions disappear. God has no hands but your hands. God has no ability but

your ability. That is what the Bible means when it says that you are God's child.

And if you look at it that way, if you set aside the idea that God is like Siri, telling you to go left or to go right, then the whole business is sacred. All of it. A pregnancy that intimates a baby is not more sacred than an abortion. You don't become sacred, like Mary, just because you conceived, and the termination of a pregnancy is not the resolution of an error. It is merely one of the reproductive outcomes. So is miscarriage. So, now, is surrogacy and in vitro fertilization—all these are on a continuum and they all hold moral weight. The God part is in your agency. The trust—the divine trust—is that you have an opportunity to participate in the population of the planet. And you have an opportunity not to participate. Is God vested one way or another in whether you, as an individual, become pregnant? No. Is a pregnancy sacred because there will be a baby, ultimately, in a bassinet, beautiful, maybe the next Obama? No. The process is bigger than you are. The part of you that's like God is the part that makes a choice. That says, *I choose to*. Or, *I choose not to*. That's what's sacred. That's the part of you that's like God to me.

The procedure room in an abortion clinic is as sacred as any other space to me, because that's where I am privileged to honor your choice. In this moment, where you need something that I am trained to give you, God is meeting both of us where we are.

Acknowledgments

I find it best to communicate from the point of view that I know best. First, the way this book happened is nothing short of miraculous, a term that I am reticent to use as a Christian because I think it is used way too much, but this time it applies. When I think about what has gone into bringing *Life's Work* to pass, my career as an obstetrician provides me with the best analogy. Between the idea of "I want to have a baby" and the day that you go home with an infant, a lot has to transpire: conception, confirmation of pregnancy, prenatal care and monitoring of well-being, labor and birth, and delivery home. The writing of a book was no less involved and, in my opinion, no less miraculous. In both scenarios the process is greatly facilitated when the right people are part of the project.

When the couples I had the privilege to care for had the idea to become pregnant, they sought out someone with my training to help them with their goal. In the case of *Life's Work*, the person I needed, providentially, found me. Rebecca Gradinger of Fletcher and Co., my agent and friend, became familiar with my story when she read "The Abortion Ministry of Dr. Willie Parker," after Mark Warren, then an editor at *Esquire*, sent John Richardson down to Mississippi to do a piece about my work. These two guys have become friends of mine, and I am grateful that they brought my work to light. I don't know why Rebecca was reading *Esquire*, a men's

213

magazine, but I'm glad she was. You know that you have the right agent when she never tries to convince you that she should be your agent. Rebecca never offered to be my agent. She only offered to help me in any way I needed her to, and accepted when I told her that I thought that she was the right person to take me on this journey. She had tracked me down, literally, by calling places that I had worked for in the past. When we began to work together, all of the dynamics in my career as an obstetrician were at play, except this time I was the person with the desire to conceive and she was the specialist to help me with it. She was my fertility specialist, helping me to conceive the idea that I had a book in me, and she helped me find a skilled writer, a literary midwife and soul mate of a friend, Lisa Miller, and her support person, Veronica Goldstein, became my literary doula, keeping us on task as we worked. With this team in place, a proposal was written and a book was conceived. I now know what my many obstetric patients felt when I helped them bring forth the thing that they nurtured inside that they cared deeply about. I am saying to you guys publicly what I hope that I conveyed to you throughout: I really appreciate you.

My newly conceived book gestating, my fertility specialist, midwife, and doula and I had to find the right literary birth attendant to deliver it, and we did that in Simon & Schuster and 37 Ink. Many great publishers were interested, but they were chosen. The 37 Ink imprint at S&S, headed by my girl, Dawn Davis, along with S&S's head of publicity, Paul Olsewski, and all of the other people at the company who became involved, came to this project on day one believing in me and what I had to say, and their enthusiasm for *Life's Work* was over the top from start to finish. I will forever be grateful for that. The miraculous part is that from the proposal pitch the first week of December 2015 to the launch date on April 4, 2017, fifteen months later, they worked with us to complete an undertaking that usually plays out over two years under the best of circumstances. S&S and 37 Ink, in a word, you guys are the bomb!

Senator Daniel Patrick Moynihan said that, "We are all entitled to our own opinions but no one is entitled to their own facts." In a period when increasingly people behave as if facts don't matter, they do. To make it clear that the facts put forth in *Life's Work* are not my own, I'm indebted to the strong work of Amy Crawford, who verified the facts on which I stand. Tasha Joyner, my assistant, also proved invaluable help in all the ways I needed.

I commit to living gratefully. Toward that end, I am naturally inclined to acknowledge everyone who ever had a kind word, a helpful action, a constructive criticism, or who patted me on the back and said, "Boy, you gon' be somebody!" However, if I did so the acknowledgments would be longer than the book. So I'll start by noting that to the people who make up the village that raised me, at every stage, I'm grateful to you even if I don't call you by name. That said, now to shout out a few people by name to the exclusion of no one:

To my siblings, Juanita, Mary, Fred, Earnestine, and Steve, and to the woman we come from, Earnestine "Jackie" Lambert: If y'all don't know how much I love you then you never will.

To my Cousin Jacqueline "Jackie" Blanks: Jackie, as I tell your daughter, little Cuz Dominique, I was your first child. I have never forgotten how you loved me and cared for me like I was you own kid when I was five and six and wanted to hop in the car with you every time it started. Thanks for the family love from then till now.

My sister from another mother: Renee "Nae" Morrow and Joseph "Joe-Joe" Foreman. Nae and Joe-Joe, we go back further than anybody that my mother didn't give birth to—since age five! I could not love you any more, even if we were blood siblings.

To my posse of "good brothas" who make me a better man: My cuz D. Wesley Poythress; Paul "PJ" Johnson; Frank "Ninja Bam-Bam" Polion; Stanley "Magic" Blackmon; George "Gee Money" Amerson; Marquis "Nube" Nuby, MD; Roderick "Rod" King, MD, MPH; Joseph "Joe B" Betancourt, MD, MPH; Hasan Davis, JD; Michael "Soul Brother #1" Thomas, MD; Luther Gaston, MD; Ronald Clarke, MD; WSP trooper Eric Purcell; and Orlando Paulding. This group is what good "men of color" look like!

Special shout-out to my CDC EIS peer and homeboy in struggle Lamar Hasbrouck, MD, MPH, author of *G-Street Lion*. Your story is a powerful one and I appreciate the brotherhood, man.

My mentors at key points in my career: at Berea College, Dr. Michael Rivage-Suel; at University of Cincinnati, Dr. Robert Rebar, Dr. Bruce Kessel, and Dr. Paula Hillard; at University of Michigan, Dr. Timothy R.B. "TJ" Johnson and Dr. Lisa Harris; and at California Department of Health Services/CDC, Dr. Gilberto "Jefe" Chavez. Professionally I stand tall on your shoulders. If I am lacking, it is my own fault.

My spiritual sherpas: Pastor Michael D. Moore, Ms. Phyllis West, and Reverend Al Miles. I have appreciated the wise counsel.

The University of Hawaii ob-gyn resident class of 2005: You women asked me to guide your training as your adviser and, through your collective principled action on behalf of women, showed me the way to my calling. Bliss Kaneshiro, MD; Reni Soon, MD; Amy Hakim, MD; Alexa Sueda, MD; Miki Yazawa Bunn, MD; and Leann Kon, MD: thank you for teaching the "teacher."

To the fierce clinic owners, most of whom are women, that I

have worked for, and to their staffs at all of the facilities where I have worked, in no particular order: Philadelphia Women's Center, Atlanta Women's Center, Jackson Women's Health Organization, Reproductive Health Services, West Alabama Women's Center, Alabama Women's Center, Family Planning Associates of Chicago, and Planned Parenthood Metropolitan of Washington. Where there are no clinics, there is no access. You all show up every day for the women of this country, mostly under thankless circumstances, in tough environments. I am proud to be in the trenches with you where the humanity of women is protected, and where you make sure that abortion is not just accessible in theory, but in practice.

Dawn Porter, JD, my first "Dawn" of my "Dawn P/Dawn D" duo. The three years shooting *Trapped* with you and the wonderful folks who worked with you were the best. That film is a real gift to women. I'm glad you stopped by the clinic that day. We got lots of work to do!

To my godchildren, Lauren Danae Poythress, Danielle Polion, and Laurel Jablonski: given that I have no biological children, you young ladies are my selfish reason for my work. I always have you in mind as I strive for reproductive and social justice. I am working for a world where you can be aware that you are female, and when that thought comes to you that it never does so as a limitation.